NEW TESTAMENT OVERVIEW IN TWENTY LESSONS

A BIBLE STUDY WORKBOOK FOR NEW-MEMBER CLASSES, BIBLE STUDY GROUPS, OR INDIVIDUALS

AN OVERVIEW OF NEW TESTAMENT DOCTRINE

Van and Barbara Ballew

PREFACE

Welcome to a new kind of Bible study
for Individuals or Groups.
As you complete these lessons, you will be expanding your ability to:
Comprehend and Interpret Scripture
Recognize Godly Principles
Love and Appreciate God's Ways
Develop a Doctrinal Base and
Appropriate the Inner Cleansing Promised In God's Word.

SOURCE MATERIAL
KING JAMES BIBLE
This version is used because it is inexpensive
and already available in most homes.

RECOMMENDATIONS FOR GROUP STUDY

This workbook is directed toward those who recently joined your church body.
Or all who desire an in-depth overview of New Testament truths.
Decide in advance whether participants will complete the lesson at home,
or complete the lesson during the first half of class time.
If class time completion works best for your group,
ask the participants to silently and independently
fill in each blank using the King James Bible.
During the second half of class time, the moderator will read each
question while encouraging the members to
share their answers and discuss the lesson's content.
The moderator will do a brief summary to conclude each class period.

THREE BOOKS IN ONE
Book I – Questions which require open Bible answers.
Book II – Overview Outline for preachers and teachers.
Book III – Answer Section to check your answers by.

Participants should pray throughout each study session, asking for revelation understanding and retention of the material covered.

TABLE OF CONTENTS

	Q	A

God's Basic Requirements:

1. God Requires Shed Blood.	1	103
2. God Requires That You Continue Believing in Jesus Christ and His Blood.	5	106

God's Higher Plan:

3. God's Higher Plan Requires "Mature Christians" – Not "Carnal Christians.	11	111
4. God's Higher Plan Requires that Christians Take Authority over Satan.	16	113
5. God's Higher Plan Requires *Agape* Love.	20	116
6. God's Higher Plan Requires Regular Church Attendance.	24	118
7. God's Higher Plan Requires Prayer.	29	121
8. God's Higher Plan Requires Patient Suffering.	33	123
9. God's Higher Plan Requires Two Kinds of Righteousness.	39	127
10. God's Higher Plan Requires Christians Who Shine For Him.	44	130
11. God's Higher Plan Requires Humility.	48	133
12. God's Higher Plan Requires Forgiving and Being Forgiven.	52	135
13. God's Higher Plan Requires Tithing.	57	138
14. God's Higher Plan Requires Two Occupied Rooms – I	62	140
15. God's Higher Plan Requires Two Occupied Rooms – II	69	145
16. How to Keep Your Soul Room Occupied for Longer Periods of Time.	73	147
17. God's Higher Plan Requires Faith -- and Acting on Your Faith.	76	149
18. God's Higher Plan Requires That You Know the Promises – And Refuse to Fear.	81	151
19. God's High Plan Requires That You Know Your Weapons.	85	153
20. God's Higher Plan Requires Three Stages of Salvation.	91	157
OVERVIEW SECTION	96	

GOD SET THREE PREREQUISITES FOR ETERNAL LIFE

1. <u>Jesus</u>, the perfect Lamb, had to become a man and shed His sinless blood for your sins.

2. <u>You</u> must believe and confess that Jesus Christ is the Son of God, and that He rose from the dead.

3. <u>You</u> must continue to believe in Jesus and the sufficiency of His blood throughout your lifetime.

FOR ADDITIONAL REWARDS, GOD HAS A DIFFERENT SET OF PREREQUISITES

As a Christian, you move into God's higher plan and become a recipient of untold rewards –
in this life and the next -- when you learn to practice the concepts in this workbook.   WELCOME!

LESSON ONE
GOD REQUIRES SHED BLOOD

Throughout these lessons you will be asked to find the stated verse and fill in each blank. Please use the King James Version because it is the version most readily available to all:

Each lesson in this workbook is entitled with a truth which every believer should know. The following verses prove the truth stated in this title.

EVIDENCE ONE:

God taught Adam His requirement for a blood sacrifice. Adam and Eve had two sons. God was pleased with Abel's blood sacrifice. God was not pleased with Cain's sacrifice because it was not the blood sacrifice which He required. Cain was so jealous of Abel that he killed him.

God said to Cain:
1. Gen.4:10 What hast thou done? The voice of thy brother's blood (1 word) _____ unto Me from the (1 word) _____

EVIDENCE TWO:

The people of Israel were God's special people; however the pharaoh in Egypt made slaves of them. The pharaoh was cruel to the Jews and made impossible demands of them, so God designed a plan to rescue His people. He then used Moses and Aaron to warn Egypt that He would kill the first son of every family if they did not allow the Israelites to return to their homeland. Pharaoh refused to free the Israelites, so God had to keep His word. To protect His special people from the curse . . .

God said to Moses:
2. Ex.12:3 Speak ye unto all the congregation of (1 word) _____.
... They shall take to them every man a (1 word) _____, a lamb ... for a house(hold).

3, Ex.12:5-6 Your lamb shall be without (1 word) _____ (imperfection) a (1 word) _____ of the first year. ... Keep it up until the (1 word) _____ day, ... and the whole assembly shall kill it in the (1 word) _____

4. Ex.12:7 And they shall take of the (1 word) _____ and strike it on the (1 word) _____ side posts and on the (1 word) _____ door post of the houses. ...

5. Ex.12:12 I (God) will pass through the land of (1 word) _____ this night and will (1 word) _____ (kill) all the firstborn in the land of Egypt. ...

6. Ex.12:13 ...And when I see the (1 word) _____ I will pass over you, and the (1 word) _____ (of death) shall not be upon (1 word) _____ ...

7. Who is our Lamb without blemish? _____

8. If animal blood protected Israel from the curse of death, Jesus' blood will protect us from the curse of punishment and death in eternal (1 word) _____

EVIDENCE THREE:

God's requirement for blood sacrifices continued from Adam up to the present time. Jesus had to complete the process by putting His own shed blood on the mercy seat in heaven thereby winning us back from Satan.

9. Heb.9:12 Neither by the blood of goats and calves, but by (Christ's) own blood, He entered in (1 word) _____ into (heaven's) holy place, having obtained (1 word) _____ redemption for (1 word) _____ ("Redemption" is Christ's having won us back from the domain of Satan which began with Adam's fall.)

EVIDENCE FOUR:

God's requirement for blood sacrifices continues now. The blood Jesus placed on the mercy seat in heaven continues to cleanse new Christians today.

10. Heb.9:22 And almost all things are by the law purged (cleansed) with (1

word) _____, and without shedding of blood is no (1 word) _____ _____. ("Remission" means complete removal. Without the shedding of Christ's blood there would be no complete removal of man's sin.)

EVIDENCE FIVE:

Jesus' blood on the mercy seat in heaven provides the way for us to enter into the very presence of God.

11. Heb.10:19-20   Having therefore, brethren, boldness to enter into the holiest by the blood of (1 word) _____, by a (1 word) _____ and living way … through the veil, that is, … His (1 word) _____. … Heb.10:22 Let us draw near (to God) with a (2 words) _____, in full assurance of (1 word) _____. …

EVIDENCE SIX:

Jesus' blood on the mercy seat in heaven will save us from God's wrath when He dispenses the final punishment on the lost.

12. Heb.10:28   He that despised Moses' law (including blood sacrifices) died without mercy under two or three (1 word) _____

13. Heb.10:29   Of how much sorer punishment … shall he be thought worthy, who hath trodden under foot the (3 words) _____ and hath counted the blood of the covenant an … (1 word) _____ thing. …

EVIDENCE SEVEN:

Jesus' blood on the mercy seat in heaven purchases our continuing right to God's forgiveness of sins.

14. Eph.1:7   In (Jesus Christ) we have (1 word) _____ through His blood, the forgiveness of (1 words) _____ according to the riches of His (1 word) _____. ("Grace" is undeserved mercy and power. This is what we receive as a result of Jesus Christ's death on the cross.)

EVIDENCE EIGHT:

Jesus' blood on the mercy seat in heaven makes us as though we had never sinned. Because of Jesus, God casts our sins into the sea of forgetfulness.

15. Rom.5:8-9 God commendeth His love toward us, in that while we were yet (1 word) _____, Christ (1 word) _____ for us. ... Being now (1 word) _____ by His blood, we shall be (3 words) _____ _____ through Him. (God sent His Son to die for us while we were still lost. His shed blood made us just as if we'd never sinned. Consequently, we shall not be part of the wrath of God which will come on the lost.)

OPEN BOOK TEST FOR LESSON ONE

16. Why was God pleased with Abel's sacrifice? (Section One) _____
_____

17. All of the animal sacrifices from the days of Adam were a foreshadow of the eventual shedding of blood by _____. His blood is the only blood which pays for man's sins.

18. Jesus' blood purchased at least six things for us. List each one: (Sections Three through Eight) _____
_____
_____
_____
_____
_____
_____
_____
_____
_____
_____
_____
_____
_____

LESSON TWO
GOD REQUIRES THAT YOU <u>CONTINUE</u> BELIEVING IN JESUS CHRIST AND HIS BLOOD

INTRODUCTION: The Bible makes it very clear that you can be truly born again, then decide to renounce Jesus Christ at a later time. You can be positive that God will never renounce you unless you first renounce His Son.

Section One
ALL CHRISTIANS BELIEVE ONE OF THESE THREE DOCTRINES:

There are denominations which teach each of the following:

A. <u>Once Saved, Always Saved:</u> (ie, These believe that no real Christian would ever turn away.)

B. <u>You Can Never Be Sure of Your Salvation:</u> (ie, These believe that we are constantly adding and subtracting "points" which will earn, or lose, their eternal life.)

C. <u>You Can Be Sure of Your Salvation--But You Can Choose To Renounce Christ:</u> (This lesson seeks to prove from the Word of God that the third doctrine is the correct one.)

RECAP: All three cannot be correct. So, which one is the true doctrine?

Section Two
THESE VERSES VERIFY THAT A CHRISTIAN CAN BE SURE OF HIS ETERNAL SALVATION:

1. I John 5:13 (John wrote): These things have I written to you that (1 word) _____ in the name of the (3 words) _____, that ye may (1 word) _____ that ye have (2 words) _____ _____, and that ye may (1 word) _____ on the name of the Son of God.

2. Gal.3:1-2 (Paul wrote to those who felt they must continue through life earning their salvation. He said): O foolish Galatians! Who hath bewitched you that ye should not obey the (1 word) _____, before whose eyes

Jesus Christ hath been evidently set forth as (1 word) _____ among you? ... Received ye the Spirit by the (1 word) _____ of the law, or by the (1 word) _____ of faith?

3. Gal.3:3 Are you so foolish? Having begun in the (born-again) (1 word) _____, are you now (being) made perfect by the (works of the) (1 word) _____?

4. Gal.4:9 ... (How is it that you) (2 words) _____ to the weak and beggarly elements, whereunto ye desire again to be in (1 word) _____?

5. Gal.5:4 Christ is become of no effect unto you. Whosoever of you are justified by the law, ye are (3 words) _____

6. Gal.5:8 This persuasion cometh not of (God) that (2 words) _____ _____. (If not from God, then it must come from Satan.)

Section Three
GOD WILL NEVER REJECT YOU,
BUT YOU CAN REJECT HIM AND HIS SON:

It is possible to be born again and later reject Jesus Christ and the Father:
7. Col.1:21-22 You that were sometimes alienated (lost), ..., yet now hath (Jesus Christ) (1 word) _____ ... through (his death), to present you (1 word) _____ and unblameable, and unreproveable in (1 word) _____ sight. (ie, You were once lost, but then you were born again.)

8. Col.1:23 (But you must) <u>continue</u> in the (1 word) _____, grounded and settled, and be not (2 words) _____ from the hope of the (1 word) _____ which ... was preached to every creature ... under heaven. ... (You must choose to never renounce the Father and the Son. Just as you were saved by audibly speaking your belief, you can be "unsaved" by audibly speaking your unbelief.)

9. Heb.2:1 Therefore we (must) give the more earnest heed to the things which

(3 words) _____, … lest we let them slip away.

10. Heb.3:12 Take heed, brethren, lest there be in any of you an evil heart of (1 word) _____, (causing you to depart) from the (2 word) _____

11. Heb.12:25 See that ye (2 words) _____ Him that (1 word) _____ (to you inside your heart.) …

<u>Section Four</u>
**WHAT CAN WE DO TO PROTECT OURSELVES
FROM EVER TURNING AWAY?**

12. Heb.12:1 … Let us (2 words) _____ every weight, and (put away) the (1 word) _____ which doth so easily beset us, and let us run with (1 word) _____ the race that is set before us. (Ask God's help as you lay aside everything that draws you away from Jesus Christ and your church family.)

13. Heb.3:6 … Hold fast the confidence and the (1 word) _____ of the hope firm unto (2 words) _____. (Do not allow Satan to send his fiery darts into your thoughts. Rejoice audibly in your confidence in Jesus Christ, and your expectation of His return.)

14. Heb.3:13 Exhort (encourage) one another daily, … lest any of you be (1 word) _____ through the deceitfulness of (1 word)_____

15. Col.1:23-24 If ye (1 word) _____ in the faith, grounded and settled, and be not (1 word) _____away from the hope of the gospel which ye have heard … I (will) rejoice in my sufferings for you. … (God's promise: Christians who remain in the Truth will never turn away.)

16. I John 2:24-25 Let that, therefore, (1 word)_____in you which ye have heard from the beginning. (If you do this), … ye also shall continue in the (1 word) _____ and in the (1 word) _____. And this is the promise that He hath promised us – even (2 words)_____

17. I John 2:23 (The Bible warns us of other religions which refuse to acknowledge the Lordship of Jesus Christ. John says): "Whosoever (3 words) _____ _____ ... hath not the Father ..."

CONCLUSION: To qualify for eternal life, a person must:
    Believe that Jesus Christ is the Son of God.
    Believe that Jesus died on the cross and rose from the dead.
    Audibly confess the above beliefs.
    Continue to believe and confess the above.
    Never audibly renounce Jesus Christ and His sacrifices.

ACCELERATED REVIEW SECTION – LESSON 2

Test your Bible maturity by doing the following. Return to:
1. **Sections 1 through 4 and**   Summarize or outline the information under each.
2. **Summarize the overall statement made by this lesson.**

_____
_____
_____
_____
_____
_____
_____
_____
_____
_____
_____
_____
_____
_____
_____
_____
_____
_____
_____
_____

TO QUALIFY FOR GOD'S <u>HIGHER</u> PLAN, A CHRISTIAN MUST DO THE FOLLOWING AS WELL:

LESSON THREE
GOD'S HIGHER PLAN REQUIRES "MATURE CHRISTIANS" – NOT "CARNAL CHRISTIANS"

INTRODUCTION: The carnal mind is diametrically opposite to the mind which follows God's leading. The carnal mind wavers between following self-thinking and Satan's darts.

Section One
WHAT IS THE CARNAL MIND?

1. Rom.8:7 The carnal mind is enmity (an enemy) against God; for it is not subject to the (3 words) _____, (ie, following God's leading) neither indeed can be.

2. Rom.8:5 For they that are (living) after the (1 word)_____ do mind the things of the flesh, but they that are after the (1 word)_____ (set their minds on) the things of the Spirit.

3. Rom.8:6 (Beware because) to be carnally minded is (1 word)_____ but to be spiritual minded is (3 words) _____

Section Two
A CARNAL MINDED CHRISTIAN HAS NOT SPENT TIME IN THE WORD:

Paul instructs these baby Christians:

4. Heb.5:12 When … ye ought to be (1 word)_____ (by this time), ye have need that one teach you again … the first (1 word)_____ of the oracles (wisdom) of God. And (you) are become such as have need of (1 word) _____ and not of strong meat. (ie, Some Christians never study the Word for themselves, always wanting someone else to feed them like babies. "Meat" means the deeper truths of God, such as you will be studying in these lessons. "Meat" also means hearing directly from God and obeying Him.)

5. Heb.6:1-2 Therefore, leaving the (baby) principles of the (1 word)_____

of Christ, let us go on to (1 word) _____ (maturity). ... (Teachers should not repeatedly teach the same few things. God's Word always provides new truths.)

6. Heb.6:11 We desire that every one of you do shew the same (1 word) _____ _____ to the full assurance of hope unto the end.

Section Three
A CARNAL MINDED CHRISTIAN IS LUKEWARM, AT BEST:

7. Rev.3:15 (Jesus said to the church at Laodicea:) "I know thy works, that thou art neither (3 words) _____. ... (Neither for or against God.)

8. Rev.3:17-18 Because thou sayest, "I am (1 word) _____ and ... have need of nothing," ... I counsel thee to buy of Me (1 word) _____ tried in the fire (a time of hardship) that thou mayest be rich and... (clothed in) (1 word) _____ raiment... . (Jesus is telling the lukewarm Christian to use the tribulation period to earn his white robe of righteousness.)

Section Four
A CARNAL MINDED CHRISTIAN DOES NOT GIVE BACK WHAT IS RIGHTFULLY GOD'S

9. Mal.3:8 Will a man (1 word) _____ God? Yet ye have robbed Me in (1 word) _____ and (1 word) _____

10. Mal.3:10-11 Bring ye all the tithes into the (1 word) _____ that there may be (1 word) _____ in Mine house, ... Prove Me now herewith, saith the Lord of hosts, if I will not open (for) you the (1 word) _____ of heaven. ... That there shall not be room enough to (1 word) _____ it. And I will rebuke the (1 word) _____ (Satan) for your sakes so that he will not destroy the (1 word) _____ of your ground. ...

Section Five
A CARNAL CHRISTIAN HAS A CARNAL MOUTH AND A CARNAL HEART:

11. Eph.4:29-30 (The Word of God says): Let no corrupt communication pro-

ceed out of your (1 word)_____, but that which is good to the use of (1 word) _____, (building up) that it may minister grace unto the hearers, and grieve not the (2 words)_____ of God. ...

12. Eph.4:31-32 Let all (1 word)_____ and wrath, and (1 word) _____, and clamor, and evil (1 word)_____ be put away from you, with all (1 word) _____ (bad intentions.) And be kind one to another, tenderhearted and forgiving one another, even as God for Christ's sake has forgiven (1 word)_____

13. Heb.12:14-15 Follow peace with all men, and holiness, without which no man shall see the (1 word) _____, looking diligently lest ... any root of (1 word)_____ springing up trouble you, and thereby many be (1 word)_____. (When division arises among Christians it affects the entire church; and some may even turn away because of it.)

Section Six
TURN FROM YOUR FORMER CARNALITY AND DO THIS:

14. Rom.12:1-2 ...Present your bodies a living (1 word) _____ holy (and) acceptable unto God, which is your reasonable (1 word)_____, and be not conformed to this world, but be ye transformed by the renewing of your (1 word)_____ that you may prove what is that good and acceptable and perfect (3 words)_____. (When you present your body and mind to do whatever God speaks to you, He will bring about His intended result. This will prove that He was the one who spoke to you and that He used you to accomplish His perfect plan.)

15. Col.3:2-3 Set your affection (desire) on things (1 word)_____, not on things on the (1 word) _____, for ye (your old man) is dead and your life is hid with (1 word)_____ in God. (You need to seek the moment-by-moment help of God and the Spirit of Christ.)

ACCELERATED REVIEW SECTION – LESSON 3

Test your Bible maturity by doing the following. Return to:

1. **Sections I through 6 and** Summarize or outline the information under each.

2. **Summarize the overall statement made by this lesson.**

LESSON FOUR
GOD'S HIGHER PLAN REQUIRES THAT CHRISTIANS TAKE AUTHORITY OVER SATAN

INTRODUCTION: God has promised to avenge us on human enemies, but we alone are responsible for dealing with Satan. We must command the devil to do what we demand, always using the name of Jesus.

Section One
PRAY THAT ALL CHRISTIANS WILL LEARN HOW TO DEFEAT SATAN:

Complete these sentences:

1. Eph.1:17 (Pray that the Father) may give unto you the spirit of (1 word) _____ and (1 word) _____ in the knowledge of Him.

2. Eph.1:18 …(Pray to be enlightened to) know the hope of His (1 word) _____ and what the riches of the (1 word) _____ of His inheritance in the saints. (Every Christian has received authority over Satan if he knows how to appropriate it.)

3. Eph,1:19-21 …(Pray that fellow-believers will) know the exceeding greatness of His (1 word) _____ to usward. (This is the same power which He wrought in Christ when) He raised Him from the dead and set Him at His own (2 words) _____, … far above all … (demonic) power and might and dominion, and every name that is named … in this (1 word) _____ and that … which is (2 words) _____

Section Two
DO YOUR JOB! TAKE AUTHORITY OVER SATAN!

When we were born again, God gave us authority in the spoken name of Jesus because:

4. Eph.2:10 We are His (1 word) _____, created in Christ Jesus unto (2 words) _____ (ie, God works) which God hath before ordained that we should walk in them.

5. Eph.3:10 (It was God's) intent that now unto the (demonic) (1 word)_____ _____ and powers in heavenly places might be known by the (1 word) _____ the manifold wisdom of God. (God asks us to demonstrate our power over Satan's entities so they will begin to tremble when a Christian opens his mouth.)

6. Eph.3:20 …He is able to do exceedingly abundantly above all that we (1 word) _____ or think, (but He is limited by the) power that worketh in (1 word) _____. (If we do not use our mouth and the name of Jesus to appropriate the power He has provided, that power lies wasted.)

Section Three
TO MAINTAIN THE HIGHEST AUTHORITY OVER SATAN, WE SHOULD DO THE FOLLOWING:

7. Eph.4:1 …Walk worthy of the (1 word) _____ with which ye were called. (ie, Recognize that Satan is your enemy. Do not go into his back yard unless called on by God to do so.)

8. Eph.4:2 (Walk) with all (3 word) _____, with longsuffering, (bearing with) one another (2 words) _____

9. Eph.4:3-4 Walk, (always) endeavoring to keep the (1 word) _____ of the Spirit, just as you were called in (2 words) _____ (and) one calling …(ie, Christians must remain in unity with their fellow-believers. We were called to this unity. If your church group is divisive and at unrest, find another church.)

10, Eph.4:13 …(because God wants His church to come into) the (4 words) _____ and of the knowledge of the (3 words) _____, to a perfect man, unto the measure of the stature of the (1 word) _____ of Christ.

11. Eph.5:6 Let no man deceive you with (2 words) _____. (It is because of empty words that the) (1 word) _____ of God cometh on the children of (1 word) _____

12. Eph.5:19-21 (Keep your heart pure by) (1 word) _____ to yourselves in psalms, hymns, and spiritual songs, making melody in your (1 word) _____ to the Lord, giving (1 word) _____ always for all things to God the Father in the (1 word) _____ of our Lord Jesus Christ, (1 word) _____ yourselves one to another in the fear of God.

Section Four
AND WE MUST . . .

13. Eph.6:10 Be strong in the Lord and in the power of (2 words) _____

14. Eph.6:13 Take unto you the whole (3 words) _____

15. I Pet.5:6 Humble yourself, therefore, under the mighty (1 word) _____ of God that he may exalt you in (2 words) _____

16. I Pet.5:7 Casting all your care upon Him for He (1 word) _____ for you.

17. I Pet.5:8 Be sober, be vigilant, because your adversary the devil … walketh about (1 word) _____ whom he may (1 word) _____

ACCELERATED REVIEW SECTION – LESSON 4

Test your Bible maturity by doing the following. Return to:
1. **Sections I through 4 and** Summarize or outline the information under each.
2. **Summarize the overall statement made by this lesson.**

_____
_____
_____
_____
_____
_____
_____
_____

LESSON FIVE
GOD'S HIGHER PLAN REQUIRES *AGAPE* LOVE

INTRODUCTION: The New Testament was written in the Greek language which has greater specificity in some of its words. For example, the Greek differentiates among the following words for "Love". (1) <u>Agape love</u> is the God-kind of love which flows from the Spirit of God within a Christian under the right conditions. (2) <u>Brotherly love</u> is love which flows from the soul.

Section One
JESUS COMMANDED CHRISTIANS TO HAVE *AGAPE* LOVE:

1. John 13:34 (Jesus said): A new (1 word) _____ I give unto you. That ye (1 word) _____ one another, as I have loved you, that ye, also love one another. (*Agape Love*)

2. John 14:23 (Jesus made this promise): … If a man *agape* love Me, he will keep (obey) My (1 word) _____; and My Father will (1 word)_____ _____ him, and We will come unto him and make our abode (2 words)___ _____. (Jesus commands that we *agape* love one another, and obey His voice. If a Christian does these two things, the Spirit of God and the Spirit of Christ will abide and work in him.)

Section Two
ONLY GOD CAN PRODUCE *AGAPE* LOVE:

3. Gal.5:22-23 (Christians cannot produce *agape* love independently of God because it is a fruit of the spirit. List the nine fruit): *Agape*_____
_____
_____

(Notice that *agape* love is the first of the fruit which God sends into your heart, soul, and mind when conditions are right. He will not send the other eight until you have met the conditions for *agape* love.)

Section Three
TO RECEIVE *AGAPE* LOVE, I MUST PREPARE MY SOUL:

4. I Pet.1:22 (Peter teaches how to prepare one's soul. He said): Seeing ye

have (1 word) _____ your souls in (1 word) _____ the truth through the spirit unto unfeigned (1 word) _____ of the brethren, see that ye (1 word) _____ one another with a (1 word) _____ heart fervently. (One way to purify your heart/soul/mind is to obey the Holy Spirit when He speaks to you. Another way is to brotherly love your fellowman; for when you do, God can use this seed to produce His fruit of *agape* love and the eight which follow.)

Section Four
WHY DOESN'T *AGAPE* LOVE FLOW
EACH TIME I FEEL BROTHERLY LOVE?

5. Heb.13:1 (The Word answers the heading's question by saying): Let brotherly love (1 word) _____. (If you do this, your seed of "continuing brotherly love" will germinate, just like any other seed.)

Section Five
HOW CAN YOU GENERATE BROTHERLY LOVE SEED?

6. Rom.12:14 (says to) (1 word) _____ them which (1 word) _____ you; bless and (1 word) _____ not. (Regardless of how someone is treating you, you must speak blessings over him. In God's mysterious way, He causes your heart to soften when you audibly speak blessings. Then, He can begin to work on the one who hurt you, because you have loosed God to work His miracle in the other person also. Use discretion. Allow the person to hear you blessing him only if the Holy Spirit gives you permission to speak in his hearing. Usually this will be done in private, repeating it until you feel a breakthrough.)

7. Eph.5:20 (tells us to be): Giving (1 word _____ always for (1 word) _____ things unto God and the Father in the (5 words) _____ _____. (When bad things happen, audibly thank God for them. Yes, <u>thank</u> Him. He did not bring the bad thing on you, but when you thank and praise Him He is in a position to move heaven and earth to ease your situation. Use discretion. This is best done in private unless the person in your presence understands this practice and will not be offended. When you have continued in brotherly love for awhile, the Spirit of God will send agape love

and the other eight spirit fruit into your heart/mind/soul.

Section Six

8. I John 2:10 He who *agape* loveth his brother abideth in the (1 word)_____ and there is none occasion of (1 word)_____ in him.

9. I John 3:14 We know that we have passed from (3 words) _____ _____, because we *agape* love the brethren. He that loveth not his brother abideth in (1 word)_____

ACCELERATED REVIEW SECTION – LESSON 5

Test your Bible maturity by doing the following. Return to:
1. **Sections I through 6 and** Summarize or outline the information under each.
2. **Summarize the overall statement made by this lesson.**

LESSON SIX
GOD'S HIGHER PLAN REQUIRES REGULAR CHURCH ATTENDANCE

INTRODUCTION: Televised messages have their place for shut-ins; but God intended that His body, the church, meet together and minister to one another as the various parts of a human body take care of the other parts.

Section One
EVERY PART OF THE BODY NEEDS EVERY OTHER PART:

1. I Cor.12:12 As the (human) body is one and hath (1 word)_____ members, and all the members of that one body, being many, are one body. So also is (1 word) _____ (who is able to be in every Christian simultaneously.)

2. I Cor.12:13 For by one Spirit are we all baptized into one (1 word)_____ whether we be Jews or (1 word) _____, ... bond or free; and have been made to drink into one (1 word) _____. (The Spirit of God baptizes all Christians into one body as part of the new birth. He provides the Spirit of Christ to give drinks of His anointing. Remember? Jesus told the woman at the well that He had water of which she knew not.)

3. I Cor.12:14-15 For the body is not one (1 word)_____, but many. If the foot shall say, "Because I am not the (1 word)_____, I am not part of the (1 word)_____; is it therefore not of the body.

4. I Cor.12:18 But now hath God set the members every one of them in the body, as it hath (2 words) _____. (We should be attending church where He sends us and serving as He leads.)

5. I Cor.12:26 Whether one member (1 word) _____, all the members suffer with it; or if one member be (1 word)_____, all the members (1 word)_____ with it. (Every church should be like this.)

6. I Cor. 12:27 Now ye are the (1 word)_____ of Christ, and members in particular.

7. I Cor.12:28 List eight ministry functions which God assigns to each church body. _____
_____
_____
(We should all be playing our part.)

Section Two
OTHER MINISTRY FUNCTIONS WE CAN QUALIFY FOR:

<u>We can walk in love toward God:</u>
8. I John 4:16 We have known and (1 word)_____ the love that God hath to us. God is (1 word)_____, and he that dwelleth in love dwelleth in (1 word)_____ and God (2 words)_____

<u>We can walk without fear:</u>
9. I John 4:18 There is no (1 word)_____ in love; but (1 word) _____ love casteth out fear; because ... He that feareth is not made (3 words) _____

<u>We can walk in love toward fellow-Christians:</u>
10. I John 4:20-21 If a man say "I (2 words)_____," and (1 word) _____ his brother, he is a (1 word)_____ .... And this command-ment have we from Him, that he who loveth (1 word)_____ love (2 words) _____ also.

<u>We can walk as led by Christ, and not as dictated by church doctrine or the law:</u>
11. Col.2:18 Let no man beguile (cheat) you of your (1 word)_____ in a voluntary (faked) (1 word)_____ and worshipping of (1 word)_____ . ... or (by being) vainly (2 words)_____ by his fleshly mind.

12. Col.2:19-20 and not holding the (1 word) _____ (Christ), from which all the body ... increaseth with the (1 word)_____ of God. Wherefore if ye be (1 word)_____ with Christ from the rudiments of the world, why ... are you subject to ordinances (the law)?

13. Col.2:23 Which things have indeed a show of wisdom in (self-will-worship), and (in) (1 word)_____, and neglecting of the (1 word)_____; not in any honor (giving in) to the satisfying of the (1 word)_____. (These things may appear to be spiritual, but they are not.)

We can work in unity within the church body:
14. Eph.4:13 (We must study the Word) till we all come in(to) the (1 word)_____ of the faith, and of the knowledge of the (3 words)_____, (growing) unto a (1 word)_____ (mature) man unto the measure of the stature of the fullness of (1 word_____

We can be sure of what we believe and why we believe it:
15. Eph.4:14 (We must study the Word and draw near to God so) that we henceforth be no more (1 word) _____ tossed to and fro, and carried about by every wind of (1 word) _____, by the sleight (trickery) of men … whereby they lie in wait to (1 word) _____

We can speak the truth in love to one another:
16. Eph.4:15-16 (We must study the Word to know <u>the truth.</u> Then we must be) speaking the (1 word)_____ in (1 word) _____ (so that we) may grow up into Him (Christ) in all things. … from whom the whole body (is) fitly (2 words)_____ … by that which every joint (1 word)_____. …

We can share our time and our resources with fellow-believers who have needs:
17. Acts 20:35 (We should follow Paul's example when he said): I have (shown) you all things … how that … ye ought to (1 word)_____ the weak and to remember the words of the Lord Jesus, how He said, (9 words)
"_____"

Section Three
BEGIN NOW TO DO THE FOLLOWING IN YOUR CHURCH:
Encourage one another:
18. Heb.3:13 Exhort one another (1 word) _____ … lest any of you be

hardened through the deceitfulness of (1 word) _____

And follow the example of the early church:
19. Acts 2:42   (Continue steadfastly) in the apostles' (1 word) _____ and (1 word) _____, and in (3 words) _____ _____ and in (1 word) _____

ACCELERATED REVIEW SECTION – LESSON 6

Test your Bible maturity by doing the following. Return to:
1. **Sections I through 3 and**   Summarize or outline the information under each.
2. **Summarize the overall statement made by this lesson.**

LESSON SEVEN
GOD'S HIGHER PLAN REQUIRES PRAYER

PRODUCTION: Pray when you are at home; pray when you go out. Pray when things look good; pray when things look bad. Paul says in I Thes.5:17 that we should pray without ceasing. Prayer takes many forms as evidenced below:

Section One
YOUR PRAYERS MUST INCLUDE PRAISE AND WORSHIP:

1. Heb.13:15 Let us offer the sacrifice of (1 word) _____ to God continually, that is, the fruit of our (1 word) _____, giving (1 word _____ to His name.

2. Phil.3:3 For we are the (true) (1 word) _____ which (1 word) _____ God in the Spirit, (1 word) _____ in Christ Jesus, and have no confidence in the (1 word) _____

3. Matt.6:9 (Jesus Himself told us to begin our prayers with worshipful praise): After this manner, therefore (1 word) _____ ye. Our Father which art in heaven, (1 word) _____ (holy and honored) be thy name. …

Section Two
YOU MUST TELL GOD WHAT YOU
NEED AND THANK HIM IN ADVANCE:

4. Phil.4:6 Be careful (anxious) for nothing, but in everything by (1word) _____ and supplication with (1 word) _____, let your requests be (2 words) _____ unto God.

5. James 4:2-3 …(If ye do not have, it is because) ye (2 words) _____ _____, … (or) because ye ask amiss (with wrong motive) that ye may consume it upon your (1 word) _____. (If you have prayed for some-thing and not received, it is because you asked for something you should not have.)

Section Three
YOU MUST INTERCEDE FOR THE NEEDS OF OTHERS,

PRAY ALL KINDS OF PRAYER, AND WAIT PATIENTLY:

6. Eph.6:18 Praying always with all (3 words) _____ in the Spirit, and watching thereunto with all (1 word) _____ _____ (patient continuance) and supplication for (2 words) _____ _____

7. Col.4:2 Continue in (1 word) _____, and watch in the same with (1 word) _____

8. I John 5:16 If any man see his brother sin a sin which is not unto (1 word) ___ _____, he shall (1 word) _____ and (God) shall give him (1 word) _____ for them. ... (However,) there is a sin unto (1 word) _____. I do not say he shall pray for it. (If a <u>very</u> mature Christian has knowingly and fully renounced Christ, the Holy Spirit will tell those who would pray for him that it is useless to do so.)

<u>Section Four</u>
YOU SHOULD OFFER UP THANKSGIVING FOR <u>ALL THINGS:</u>

9. Eph.5:20 (The Word instructs Christians to be) giving (1 word) _____ always for (2 words) _____ unto God and the Father, in the name of our (3 words) _____

10. I Thes.5:16-18 Rejoice (1 word) _____! Pray (2 words) _____. In everything (2 words) _____ _____ for this is the (3 words) _____ in Christ concerning you.

11. Rom.8:28 (This is the promise God has for those who are thankful in all circumstances): And we know that all things (will) work together for (1 word) _____ to them that (1 word) _____ God, to them who are (2 words) _____ according to His purpose. (This is God's promise: If you will thank Him in all circumstances, He will see that everything in life will work to your good.)

<u>Section Five</u>
YOU MUST SPEAK IN FAITH:

12. Eph.6:16 Above all, taking the shield of (1 word)_____ wherewith ye shall be able to quench all the (2 words)_____ of the wicked (one).

13. I Pet.5:6-7 Humble yourselves therefore under the mighty (1 word)_____ _____ of God that He may (1 word) _____ you in due time.

14. I Pet.5:8-9 (Be) (1 word) _____, be (1 word)_____; because your adversary the (1 word)_____, as a roaring (1 word)_____ walketh about, seeking whom he may (1 word)_____. Whom resist, steadfast in the (1 word) _____ knowing that the same afflictions (problems) are accomplished in your brethren that are (3 words)_____
_____

15. Matt.18:18 Jesus said: …Whatsoever ye shall (1 word)_____ on earth shall be (1 word) _____ in heaven; and whatsoever ye shall (1 word) _____ on earth shall be loosed in (1 word)_____

ACCELERATED REVIEW SECTION – LESSON 7

Test your Bible maturity by doing the following. Return to:
1. **Sections I through 5 and**   Summarize or outline the information under each.
2. **Summarize the overall statement made by this lesson.**

_____
_____
_____
_____
_____
_____
_____
_____
_____
_____
_____
_____

LESSON EIGHT
GOD'S HIGHER PLAN REQUIRES PATIENT SUFFERING

INTRODUCTION: Patience is a virtue highly esteemed by our Father. This is a study of patient suffering.

Section One
GOD IS OUR EXAMPLE OF PATIENCE, AS FOLLOWS:

1. Rom.2:4 (The Word says): Despiseth thou the riches of His (1 word)_____ and (1 word)_____ (patience) and (1 word)_____; not knowing that the goodness of God leadeth thee to (1 word)_____. (God is our model of patience. He patiently waits for a person to turn to Him, thereby giving sufficient time for repentance.)

2. 2 Pet.3:15 Account that the longsuffering of our Lord is (1 word)_____ – even as our beloved brother (1 word)_____ ... hath written unto you. (ie, Because of God's patience, many come to Christ and grow into maturity. When you are patient in the midst of sufferings, people will see Christ in you.)

3. Rom.9:22-23 What if God, willing to show His wrath (on the lost) and to make His (1 word)_____ known, endured with much longsuffering the vessels of wrath fitted to destruction (so) that He might make known the (1 word)_____ of His glory on the vessels of mercy. ... (God does not take quick vengeance on the lost. Instead He allows the human race to continue in its ways so that those who are willing can come to Him.)

4. Rom.15:5 Now (may) the God of (1 word)_____ and (1 word)_____ grant you to be likeminded one toward another, according to Christ Jesus. (We must be patient and nurturing with others just as God and Jesus are patient and nurturing with us.)

Section Two
GOD ASKS US TO PRACTICE PATIENCE ALSO:

5. Luke 8:15 (God says that "good grounds" are): they which (hear with) an

(1 word) _____ and (1 word) _____ heart, (and) having heard the Word, keep it and bring forth fruit with (1 word) _____. (A believer who has an honest and good heart will see his prayers answered if he continues to believe with patience.)

6. Luke 21:19 In your (1 word) _____ (you will be able to) (1 word) _____ your souls. (ie, A person who can control his feelings while remaining patient is having control over his soul and thereby saving it.)

7. James 1:4 (The Word says that you must) let (1 word) _____ have her perfect work, that ye may be (1 word) _____ and entire, wanting nothing. (ie, If a Christian can practice patience, he will be moving toward maturity.)

8. Eph.4:1-3 (The Word urges Christians to) (1 word) _____ worthy of the vocation wherewith ye are (1 word) _____, with all lowliness and meekness, with (1 word) _____, forbearing one another in (1 word) _____ _____, endeavoring to keep the (1 word) _____ of the Spirit in the bond of (1 word) _____

9. 2 Thes.3:5 (You can remain patient and unified in love only with the help of God, so we pray: May) the Lord (1 word) _____ your hearts into the love of God and into the patient (1 word) _____ _____ for Christ.

10. I Tim.6:6 (Remember this): Godliness with (1 word) _____ is great (1 word) _____. (Godliness and contentment can be sustained only by patient endurance.)

11. Heb.10:36 For ye have need of (1 word) _____ (so) that after ye have done the will of God, ye may receive the (1 word) _____. (It is God's will that you wait patiently while the promises are on their way to you.)

12. James 5:7 Be (1 word) _____, therefore, brethren, unto the (1

word) _____ of the Lord. ...

13. James 5:8 Be ye also (1 word) _____, establish your (1 word) _____, for the coming of the Lord draweth nigh.

Section Three
FAITH MUST BE ADDED TO PATIENCE:

14. Heb.6:12 (The Word says): that ye be not slothful (sluggish and lazy), but be followers of them who through (1 word) _____ and patience inherit the (1 word) _____. (You should be familiar with the Bible heroes and follow their example.)

15. Tit.2:1-2 (You must): (1 word) _____ thou the things which become sound doctrine. (We must encourage) the aged men (to) be sober, grave, temperate, sound in (1 word) _____, in (1 word) _____, in (1 word) _____

16. Phil.4:6-7 (The Word says to): be (1 word) _____ (anxious) for nothing, but in everything, by (1 word) _____ and supplication, with (1 word) _____, let your requests be made known unto God; and the (1word) _____ of God which passeth all understanding, shall keep your(1 word) _____ and (1 word) _____ through Christ Jesus. (Speak rebuke to fear and anxiety – in the name of Jesus.)

17. 2 Pet.1:5-7 And beside this, giving all (1 word) _____, add to your faith (1 word) _____; and (add) to your virtue (1 word) _____; and (add) to your knowledge (1 word) _____ (self-control); and (add) to your temperance (1 word) _____; and (add) to your patience (1 word) _____; and (add) to godliness brotherly kindness; and (add) to brotherly kindness (1 word) _____ (All of these attributes issue from a pure heart. Purity of heart is essential to successful Christian living.)

Section Four

FAITH PLUS PATIENCE EQUALS "HOPE":
18. Rom.8:25 (God says): If we (1 word) _____ for that we see not, then do we with (1 word) _____ wait for it.

Section Five
KNOW THAT GODLY PEOPLE WILL SUFFER AT TIMES:
19. 2 Tim.3:12 (Paul told Timothy): ... all that will live (1 word) _____ in Christ Jesus shall suffer (1 word) _____

20. 2 Thes.1:4 (Paul told the churches of God: We glory in you for your) (1 word) _____ and (1 word) _____ in all your (1 word) _____ and tribulations that ye endure).

Section Six
YOU MUST REJOICE DURING SUFFERINGS:
21. James 1:2-3 My brethren, (4 words) _____ when ye fall into diverse (1 word) _____, knowing this, that the trying of your (1 word) _____ worketh (1 word) _____. (When you fall into trials, audibly rejoice! God will reward this.)

22. I Pet.1:6-7 Wherein ye greatly (1 word) _____, though now for a season, if need be, ye are in heaviness through manifold (1 word) _____ that the trial of your (1 word) _____ ... might be found unto (1 word) _____ and (1 word) _____ and glory at the appearing of Jesus Christ (at the rapture).

23. Eph.5:20 Giving (1 word) _____ always for (2 words) _____ unto God and the Father in the (1 word) _____ of our Lord Jesus Christ. (Audibly thank God, regardless of how things look around you.)

24. Rom.12:14 (And) (1 word) _____ them which (1 word) _____ you; bless and curse not.

ACCELERATED REVIEW SECTION – LESSON 8

Test your Bible maturity by doing the following. Return to:

1. **Sections I through 6 and** Summarize or outline the information under each.

2. **Summarize the overall statement made by this lesson.**

LESSON NINE
GOD'S HIGHER PLAN REQUIRES TWO KINDS OF RIGHTEOUSNESS

INTRODUCTION: Why does God require shed blood and belief in Jesus Christ for all, yet He has a Higher Plan which all Christians should press toward? The answer to that question is that God has two kinds of righteousness. The first kind of righteousness is the "Righteousness of God". The second kind of righteousness is the "Righteousness of Christ" This is a study of the two, their meanings, and their rewards.

Section One
THE "RIGHTEOUSNESS OF GOD" IS THE "NEW BIRTH":
The new birth is available only through belief in the shed blood of Christ:

1. John 3:3 (Jesus said): ... I say unto thee, except a man is (2 words)_____ _____, he cannot see the (3 words)_____

2. John 3:5 (Jesus added): ... Except a man is born of (1 word) _____ and of the (1 word) _____, he cannot enter into the kingdom of God. (There are two ways of understanding this verse: Born of water can mean being physically birthed from your mother; or it can mean being born again by hearing, believing, and confessing the gospel of Christ. The Word is referred to as washing water throughout the New Testament. To be born the second time is to accept Jesus Christ as your Savior. Unless the new birth occurs, you will not/cannot go to heaven and live eternally with God and Jesus Christ.)

Section Two
HOW IS THE NEW BIRTH ACCOMPLISHED?

3. Rom.10:9-10 ...If thou shalt (1 word) _____ with thy mouth the Lord Jesus and shalt (1 word) _____ in thine heart that God hath (2 words) _____ from the dead, thou shalt be saved. For with the (1 word) _____ man believeth unto righteousness; and with the (1 word)_____ confession is made unto salvation. (A person is born again and receives the righteousness of God by having faith in Jesus Christ and confessing his belief audibly.)

Section Three
OTHER SCRIPTURE WHICH SPEAK OF THE
NEW BIRTH RIGHTEOUSNESS OF GOD:

4. Rom.3:20-22 Therefore, by the deeds of the (1 word) _____ there shall no flesh be justified in His sight. For by the law is (merely) the (1 word) _____ of sin. But now the righteousness of God without the law is manifested, being witnessed by the law and the prophets. Even the righteousness of God which is by (1 word) _____ of Jesus Christ. ...

5. Rom.1:16-17 (Paul said): ... I am not ashamed of the gospel of Christ, for it is the (1 word) _____ of God unto salvation to everyone that (1 word) _____. ... (For in the gospel of Christ) is the righteousness of God revealed from (3 words) _____. ... The just shall (1 word) _____ by faith.

6. Rom.10:3 (Israel refused the new birth righteousness of God when they crucified the Messiah.) For they being ignorant of God's righteousness, and going about to (1 word) _____ their own righteousness, have not (1 word) _____ themselves to the righteousness of God. (If you have been born again, you are a true Christian. If you have not taken this critical step, take a moment and appropriate Romans 10:9-10 above. You must audibly confess your acceptance of Jesus Christ as the risen Son of God. Just as God spoke the worlds into place. We speak our new world into place.)

Section Four
THE NEW BIRTH OCCURS IN MAN'S SPIRIT:

Man is spirit, soul, and body: The new birth occurs in the innermost part of man, called the spirit. When you confess Jesus Christ as described above, the Spirit of God comes and dwells in your new spirit. The born-again spirit cannot sin.

7. I Cor. 3:16 Know ye not that ye are the (3 words) _____ _____, and that the (3 words) _____ dwelleth in you? (Old Testament believers were incapable of having the righteousness of God because the Spirit of God could not dwell in mankind before Jesus paid the price with His blood.)

Section Five
THE "RIGHTEOUSNESS OF CHRIST" IS THE RENEWING OF THE SOUL:

The soul is the second part of mankind: The soul consists of a person's heart and mind. When the Word speaks of heart, mind, or soul, it is referring to the soul of man.

8. 3 John 2 (God wants the soul of every Christian to prosper. John, the apostle, wrote): Beloved, I wish (3 words) _____ that thou mayest prosper and be in health, even as thy (1 word) _____ prospereth. (Any physician can tell you that a heart and mind at peace is much more likely to have a healthy body and a productive life.)

Section Six
VERSES ABOUT THE "RIGHTEOUSNESS OF CHRIST":

Match each verse to its proper address:

____ 9. I die to the law that I might live to God's voice.   A. Col.2:6-7

____ 10. You have a choice: Either yield your body to righteousness or to iniquity.   B. Gal.2:20

____ 11. Righteousness by faith is a day-by-day goal.   C. Gal.2:19

____ 12. The righteousness of Christ is attained through walking by faith in Jesus Christ.   D. Gal.3:5

____ 13. God is able to minister to you and work miracles through your faith, not the law.   E. Rom.6:19

____ 14. When I crucify myself, Christ lives in and through me.   F. Gal.5:5

Section Seven
OLD TESTAMENT RIGHTEOUSNESS OF CHRIST:

The Righteousness of Christ was available in the Old Testament because man has always had a soul:

15. Gen.2:7 The Lord God (1 word) _____ man of the dust of the ground, and (1 word) _____ into his nostrils the breath of life, and man became a living soul (or living being).

16. Heb.11:7 (Noah is one of many Old Testament saints who were accounted as having the righteousness of Christ.) By (1 word) _____ Noah ... prepared an ark to the saving of his house, by the which he condemned the world, and became (1 word) _____ of the righteousness which is by (1 word) _____

ACCELERATED REVIEW SECTION – LESSON 9

Test your Bible maturity by doing the following. Return to:
1. **Sections I through 7 and** Summarize or outline the information under each.
2. **Explain "the righteousness of God".**
3. **Explain "the righteousness of Christ".**
4. **Summarize the overall statement made by this lesson.**

_____
_____
_____
_____
_____
_____
_____
_____
_____
_____
_____
_____
_____
_____
_____

LESSON TEN
GOD'S HIGHER PLAN REQUIRES CHRISTIANS WHO SHINE FOR HIM

INTRODUCTION: If you are a Christian, you are a lighthouse. Is your light shining bright? Can others find their way by keeping their eyes on you? The purpose of this lesson is to teach every Christian to become high voltage, bright lighthouses for those around them.

Section One
TO BECOME A SHINING LIGHTHOUSE, DO THE FOLLOWING:
Determine you want to be the light of Christ and not self. Seek His leading and you will shine like a beacon.

1. John 8:12 (Jesus said): I am the (1 word)_____ of the world. He who followeth Me shall not walk in (1 word)_____ _____ but shall have the (3 words)_____. (Determine to use Jesus as your role model. He repeatedly said that He did nothing but what the Father told him to do.)

Eliminate complaining and disputing from your life, and hold fast to the truth that is in Jesus Christ and His Word.

2. Phil.2:14-16 (The Word teaches): Do all things without (3 words)_____ _____ that ye may be blameless and harmless, the (3 words)_____ without rebuke in the midst of a crooked and perverse nation among whom ye (1 word)_____ as lights in the (1 word)_____. ("Murmering" is complaining)

Monitor your thoughts and your behavior.

3. I Thes.5:4-6 But ye, brethren, are not in (1 word)_____, that that day should overtake you as a (1 word)_____. Ye are all the children of (1 word)_____; we are not of the (1 word)_____ or darkness. Therefore, let us not sleep ... but let us watch and be (1 word)_____

Practice "Faith plus Hope equals *Agape* Love" to appropriate Holy Spirit oil.

4. I Thes.5:8-9 Let us who are of the (1 word) _____ be sober, putting on the breastplate of (3 words) _____, and for an helmet the (1 word) _____ of salvation by our Lord Jesus Christ. (A breastplate covers both the spirit and soul of a Christian. Thus, the words used to fill in these blanks list the elements of a breastplate of righteousness.)

Keep your armor in place.

5. Eph.6:13 …Take unto you the whole armor of God, that you may be able to (1 word) _____ in the evil day, and having done (1 word) _____ (the Word tells you to do), to stand.

6. Eph.6:14 Stand therefore, having your loins girt about with (1 word) _____, and having on the (3 words) _____ _____. (The truth is God's Word – what He speaks to you and what He has written in Scripture. You "stand" when you know and practice "the truth" and your spirit and soul are covered with the breastplate of righteousness.)

7. Eph.6:15 (Shod your feet) with the preparation of the gospel of (1 word) _____. (God's truth is a message of peace. You must know God's words about peace and walk accordingly.)

8. Eph.6:16 Above all, taking the shield of (1 word) _____ wherewith ye shall be able to quench all the (2 words) _____ of the wicked (one). (Satan puts wicked thoughts into your mind, and he uses his people to send tribulation into your life.)

9. Eph.6:17 And take the helmet of (1 word) _____ (a renewed mind.) and the sword of the Spirit which is the (3 words) _____ _____. (When a believer speaks the Word of God with authority, using the name of Jesus, the spoken words act as a sword to cut away Satan's attacks.)

10. Eph.6:18 Praying always with all (kinds of) (1 word) _____

and supplication in the Spirit, and (1 word) _____ thereunto with all perseverance and supplication for all saints. (Pray in the Spirit, and pray for your fellow-believers.)

Section Two
WHAT MUST WE DO TO KEEP OUR LAMPS FULL?

Continually give praises to God, knowing that the oil comes from the Holy Spirit and not from yourself.

11. Col.1:12 (Your lamp shines when you thank Him): Giving (1 word) _____ _____ unto the Father, which has made us meet to be partakers of the inheritance of the saints in (1 word) _____. (When you speak thanksgivings to God, your light turns on and you become a recipient of the promises due to those who walk in the light.)

Share your blessings with others while deflecting all glory onto the Father and the Son – never keep it for yourself.

12. Matt.5:14 (Jesus said): Ye are the (1 word) _____ of the world. A city that is set on a hill cannot be hid. (A person whose light is shining is as apparent to others as a city sitting on a hill.)

13. Matt.5:16 Let your light so (1 word) _____ before men, that they may see your good works and (1 word) _____ your Father which is in heaven. ("Good works" are works which a Christian does in obedience to God's voice. When others notice, you must be sure that you deflect all glory to God, and not self.)

Stay in the word daily. The word creates oil for your lamp/lighthouse.

14. Luke 12:35 (Jesus said): Let your loins be girded about (with the truth), and your (2 words) _____

15. Luke 11:35 (Jesus also said): Take heed therefore that the (1 word) _____ _____ which is in thee is not (1 word) _____. (Do not attempt to fake light; otherwise you produce darkness. The Spirit within you is the source of true light.)

ACCELERATED REVIEW SECTION – LESSON 10

Test your Bible maturity by doing the following. Return to:

1. **Sections I through 2 and** Summarize or outline the information under each.
2. **Summarize the overall statement made by this lesson.**

LESSON ELEVEN
GOD'S HIGHER PLAN REQUIRES HUMILITY

INTRODUCTION: Individuals, as well as nations, must humble themselves before God.

Section One
WHAT MUST A NATION DO?

1. 2 Chron.7:14 (God says): If My people which are called by My name shall (1 word) _____ themselves and (1 word) _____ and (1 word) _____ My face and (1 word) _____ from their wicked ways, then will I (1 word) _____ from heaven, and will forgive their sin and will (1 word) _____ their land.

Section Two
GOD SAYS WE MUST HUMBLE OURSELVES:•

Because pride deceives the heart:

2. Oba.1:3 (God says): The pride of thine heart hath (1 word) _____ thee, thou that dwelleth in the clefts of the rock, whose habitation is (1 word) _____, that saith in his heart, Who shall bring me (1 word) _____ _____ to the ground.

Because pride in the heart defiles the whole man:

3. Mark 7:20-23 (Jesus says): That which cometh (2 words) _____ _____ the man, that (1 word) _____ the man. For from within, out of the heart of men, proceed (2 words) _____, etc. ... All these evil things come from (1 word) _____ and defile the man.

Because pride of heart is worldly:

4. I John 2:16 For all that is in the world -- the lust of the (1 word) _____, and the lust of the (1 word) _____, and the (1 word) _____ of life is not of the Father, but is of the (1 word) _____

And: Because pride brings destruction and failure:

5. Prov.16:18 Pride goeth before (1 word) _____, and a haughty spirit before a (1 word) _____

6. Prov.16:19 Better it is to be of a (1 word) _____ spirit with the lowly than to divide the spoil with the (1 word) _____

<u>The humble are more likely to be rich in faith:</u>
7. James 2:5 …Hath not God chosen the (1 word) _____ of this world (to be) rich in (1 word) _____ and heirs of the kingdom which hath He promised to them that (1 word) _____ Him. (God chose the poor to be the primary recipient of His grace.)

8. James 4:6 God resisteth the (1 word) _____, but giveth grace to the (1 word) _____

9. James 4:10 (So) (1 word) _____ yourselves in the sight of the Lord, and He shall (3 words) _____

<u>The humble are in a position to be exalted:</u>
10. I Pet.5:6 (God says): Humble yourselves therefore under the mighty hand of God, that (1 word) _____ may exalt you in due time.

<u>The humble increase their joy:</u>
11. Isa.29:19 The meek also shall (1 word) _____ their joy in the Lord, and the (1 word) _____ among men shall rejoice in the Holy One of Israel.

<u>The humble Christian will walk as follows:</u>
12. Eph.4:1-3 … Walk worthy of the vocation wherewith ye are called, with all (1 word) _____, with longsuffering, (1 word) _____ one another in love, endeavoring to keep the unity of the Spirit in the (1 word) _____ of peace.

13. Rom.12:2 And be not conformed to this (1 word) _____, but be ye (1 word) _____ by the (1 word) _____ of your mind, that you may prove what is that good and acceptable and perfect (3 words) ____
_____

Page 49

Section Three
GOD PLEADS WITH YOU TO COME TO HIM IN HUMILITY:

<u>Sincere prayer is evidence of humility:</u>
14. Matt. 26:41 (Jesus said): (1 word) _____ and (1 word) _____, that ye enter not into temptation. (When you pray, you demonstrate your dependence on God.)

<u>Confession of sins is evidence of humility:</u>
15. I John 1:9   For if we (1 word) _____ our sins, He is faithful and just to (1 word) _____ us our sins and to (1 word) _____ us from all unrighteousness.

ACCELERATED REVIEW SECTION – LESSON 11

Test your Bible maturity by doing the following. Return to:
1. **Sections I through 3 and** Summarize or outline the information under each.
2. **List seven reasons why a Christian should remain humble.**
3. **Summarize the overall statement made by this lesson.**

LESSON TWELVE
GOD'S HIGHER PLAN REQUIRES FORGIVING AND BEING FORGIVEN

INTRODUCTION: A pure heart is a heart which rests in peace and goodwill toward God and others. God desires that every Christian walk in peace.

Section One
SCRIPTURE REQUIRING GOODWILL TOWARD OTHERS:
1. Col.3:12 Put on therefore, as the elect of God, holy and beloved, bowels of (1 word) _____, (and) (1 word) _____, humbleness of mind, meekness, (and) longsuffering.

Section Two
SCRIPTURE REQUIRING FORGIVENESS TOWARD OTHERS:
2. Col.3:13 Forbearing one another and (1 word) _____ if any man have a quarrel against any; even as (2 words) _____ you, so also do ye.

Section Three
SCRIPTURE REQUIRING GOODNESS TOWARD OTHERS:
3. Col.3:14 And above all these things put on (1 word) _____, which is the bond of perfection.

Section Four
SCRIPTURE REQUIRING A HEART OF PEACE:
4. Col.3:15 And let the (3 words) _____ rule in your hearts, to the which also ye (2 words) _____ in one body; and be ye (1 word) _____

Section Five
WHAT DID JESUS TEACH ABOUT FORGIVENESS?
5. Matt.18:21 (Peter came to Jesus and said): "Lord, how oft shall my brother sin against me, and I (2 words) _____? Till (1 word) _____ times?"

6. Matt.18:22 (Jesus answered): "I say <u>not</u> unto thee, "Until seven times; but (I say) "Until (3 words) _____. (I must forgive

without end, both for the offender's sake and mine.)

7. Mark 11:25-26 (Jesus said): And when ye stand praying, (1 word)_____ _____, if ye have aught against any; (3 words)_____ _____ also which is in heaven (2 words)_____ you your trespasses. But if ye do not (1 word) _____, neither will your Father which is in heaven (3 words)_____

Section Six
WHAT DID JESUS TEACH ABOUT CLEARING A DISAGREEMENT WITH A FELLOW CHRISTIAN?

8. Luke 17:3-4 (When you are sure you have forgiven your brother, but he continues to be offending, you may do the following): Take heed to yourselves. (Get your heart right!) If thy brother trespass against thee, (2 words) _____; and if he repent, (2 words)_____ _____. -- (Tell him what he is repeatedly doing that is hurtful to you.) If he repents, (tell him you) forgive him.

9. Luke 17:5 (The apostles felt this was humanly impossible, so they said to the Lord): (3 words) _____. (If forgiveness seems too difficult for you as well, pray these words from the apostles.)

10. Luke 17:6 (So, Jesus taught the apostles how to increase their faith and see their unforgiveness disappear.) If ye had (1 word) _____ as a grain of mustard seed, ye might (1 word)_____ unto the sycamine tree, (representing unforgiveness), "Be thou (2 words) _____ by the root, and be thou (1 word) _____ in the sea, and it should obey you. (Say, " In the precious name of Jesus Christ, I command Satan and his unforgiveness to leave my body and be cast into the sea.")

11. Matt.5.44 (Jesus said): ... Love your (1 word) _____. Bless them that (1 word) _____ you. Do (1 word) _____ to them that hate you, and (1 word) _____for them which despitefully use you and persecute you.

Section Seven

WHAT ELSE DID JESUS TEACH ABOUT DISPUTES?

12. Matt.18:15 (Jesus said): ... If thy brother shall (1 word) _____ against thee, (ie, takes your property or harms it), go and (2 words) _____ _____ his fault between thee and him alone. If he shall hear thee (and replaces your property), thou hast gained thy brother.

13. Matt.18:16 But if he will not (1 word) _____ thee, then take with thee one or two more (who are witnesses to the crime) that in the (1 word) _____ of two or three witnesses, (2 words) _____ _____ (you say) may be (1 word) _____.

14. Matt.18:17 And if he shall (1 word) _____ to hear them, tell it unto the church (leadership). But if he neglect to hear the (1 word) _____ _____ let him be unto thee as an (1 word) _____ man and a publican. (The Old Testament Jews were allowed to take foreigners and tax collectors before governmental judges. The Christian is permitted to take the offender to court at this point.)

15. I Cor.6:7 (Paul taught that it is a no-win situation for all if a Christian takes a brother before a heathen court. He said): ... Why do you not rather suffer yourselves to be (1 word) _____

Section Eight
TO ACCOMPLISH TRUE FORGIVENESS WITHIN
THE HEART – SPEAK BLESSINGS ON THE OFFENDER:

16. Matt.5:44 (Jesus said): ... (1 word) _____ them that curse you, (2 words) _____ to them that hate you, and (2 words) _____ _____ them that spitefully use you.

Section Nine
TO ENSURE THAT GOD CONTINUES TO FORGIVE
YOUR SINS – CONFESS EACH SIN TO HIM

17. I John 1:9 If we (1 word) _____ our sins, he is faithful and just to (2 words) _____ our sins, and , and to (2 words) _____ _____ from all unrighteousness.

ACCELERATED REVIEW SECTION – LESSON 12

Test your Bible maturity by doing the following. Return to:
1. **Sections I through 9 and** Summarize or outline the information under each.
2. **Summarize the overall statement made by this lesson.**

LESSON THIRTEEN
GOD'S HIGHER PLAN REQUIRES TITHING

INTRODUCTION: Are you financially strapped? God's Word has the answer to every solution. He desires to see His children prosper, and his Word tell us how.

Section One
IF YOU DESIRE TO PROSPER FINANCIALLY YOU MUST PLANT YOUR TITHE SEED EVERY WEEK:

1. Mal.3:10 (God's Word says): Bring ye all the (1 word) _____ into the storehouse that there may be meat in My (1 word) _____. Prove Me now herewith, saith the Lord, …if I will not open you the windows of (1 word) _____ and pour you out a blessing, that there shall not be room enough to receive it.

2. Mal.3:11 (When you give to God, He promises to): (3 words) _____ _____ (Satan) for your sakes, so that he will not destroy the (1 word) _____ of your ground.

Section Two
IF YOU ARE NOT TITHING, PRAY FOR STRENGTH TO START:

3. I Cor.2:5 (Pray) that your (1 word) _____ should not stand in the wisdom of men, but in the (3 words) _____

4. James 1:5-6 (Pray for wisdom to know what to pray, because): If any of you lack wisdom, let him (3 words) _____ that giveth to all men liberally and upbraideth not; and it shall be given him. … But let him (3 words) _____ … .

5. I Cor.1:25 (Recognize the need for God's help, because): the foolishness of God is (1 word) _____ than men; and the weakness of God is (1 word) _____ than men.

6. I Cor.1:30a Of Him are ye in Christ Jesus, who … is made unto us (1 word) _____ and righteousness and sanctification and redemption.

7. I Cor.3:19 For the wisdom of this (1 word) _____ is (1 word) _____ with God.. ..

Section Three
YOU MUST CURB YOUR WASTEFUL SPENDING BY:
8. Col.3:16 (Letting) the (3 words) _____ dwell in you richly in all wisdom. ... (ie, Stay in the Word.)

Section Four
CURB YOUR SPENDING BY THANKING GOD FOR THE THINGS YOU HAVE NOW:
9. Psa.100:2 (The Word says to): Serve the Lord with (1 word) _____ _____; come before His presence with (1 word) _____

10. Col.3:15 And let the peace of God rule in your (1 word) _____, to the which …ye are (1 word) _____ … and be thankful.

11. Eph.5:20 Giving thanks always for (1 word) _____ things unto God …in the (1 word) _____ of our Lord Jesus Christ.

12. Phil.4:6 (We are told to never worry), but in every thing, by (1 word) ____ _____ and supplication, with (1 word) _____, let your requests be made known unto God.

13. Heb.13:15 By Him therefore, let us offer the sacrifice of (1 word) _____ _____ to God (1 word) _____, ... giving thanks to His name.

14. 2 Cor.2:14 Now thanks be unto God which always causeth us to us (1 word) _____ in Christ ...

15. I Cor.15:57 But (1 word) _____ be to God which giveth us the (1 word) _____ through our Lord Jesus Christ.

Section Five
COMMIT TO PRACTICING SELF-CONTROL THAT:

16. 2 Pet.1:4-8 …ye might be partakers of the (2 words) _____ _____; having escaped the corruption that is in the world through (1 word) _____

17. I Pet.2:11 …Fleshly lusts war against the (1 word) _____

Section Six
COMMIT TO SHARE WITH THOSE IN NEED:
18. Eph.4:28 (Do not steal. Work with your hands that you) may have something (2 words) _____ to him that (1 word) _____

Section Seven
I COMMIT TO THE FOLLOWING PRIORITIES:
19. I will give God the first ten percent every week.

20. I will put ten percent in savings every week, and live on the remaining eighty percent.

21. My gifts to others will come out of my living allowance or savings account.

ACCELERATED REVIEW SECTION – LESSON 13
Test your Bible maturity by doing the following. Return to:
1. **Sections I through 7 and** Summarize or outline the information under each.
2. **Summarize the overall statement made by this lesson.**
3. **List twenty things for which you should be thanking God. (Then do it!)**

_____
_____
_____
_____
_____
_____
_____
_____

LESSON FOURTEEN
GOD'S HIGHER PLAN REQUIRES TWO OCCUPIED ROOMS -- I

INTRODUCTION: If you are a Christian, you are the living, breathing temple of God. You are His three-part tabernacle on earth. You are spirit, soul, and body. Heaven's plan is: That the Spirit of God occupy your spirit room; that the Spirit of Christ occupy your soul room; and that you occupy and master your flesh with God's help.

Section One
THIS IS HOW THE OLD TESTAMENT TABERNACLE LOOKED:
(The outer court is not pictured in Sections One and Two.)

HOLY PLACE	MOST HOLY PLACE

Section Two
THIS IS HOW (YOU) THE NEW TESTAMENT TABERNACLE LOOKS TO GOD:

HEART MIND (SOUL)	BORN AGAIN (SPIRIT)

Section Three
INFORMATION ABOUT THE CHRISTIAN'S SPIRIT:
Your new spirit was prophesied by Jeremiah and described in Hebrews:
1. Heb.8:10 …(God promised to put His laws in their) (1 word) _____ and write them in their (1 word) _____; and I will be to them a God and they shall be to Me a (1 word) _____

God's Spirit cannot dwell in a person until God prepares a new place for His Spirit:

Jesus taught about the change which comes about as soon as a person asks Jesus Christ to be his personal Lord and Savior.

2. Mark 2:22 ... No one putteth new (1 word) _____ into old bottles; else the new wine doth burst the bottles, and the wine is spilled, and the bottles will be marred; but (2 words) _____ must be put into (2 words) _____. (You new spirit place is the new bottle. God's Spirit is the new wine.)

When the new place has been prepared, the Spirit of God comes in and the new **birth occurs. All this can happen in a moment's time:**

3. I Cor.3:16 Know ye not that ye are the (3 words) _____ _____, and that the Spirit of God dwelleth in (1 word) _____?

The Spirit of God will speak to you from within your new spirit. Your job is to listen and obey:

4. Rom.8:14 For as many as are (1 word) _____ by the Spirit of God, they are sons of (1 word) _____

The moment you are born again, you are pure throughout your spirit and soul, regardless of your past:

5. I Cor.6:11 Paul said: (You were many evil things before), but ye are washed, but ye are sanctified (set apart for God's use), but ye are justified in the (1 word) _____ of the Lord Jesus Christ, and by the (1 word) _____ of our God.

As a born-again Christian, you have access to the following promise:

6. I Cor.6:12 ...All things are (1 word) _____ for me, but I will not be brought under the (3 words) _____

Section Four
INFORMATION ABOUT THE CHRISTIAN'S SOUL:

Three words refer to all, or part, of the soul of man:

You are responsible for keeping your <u>heart/mind/soul</u> clean so that God can use you:

THE MIND:

7. Rom.12:2 Be not conformed to this (1 word) _____, but be ye transformed by the renewing of your (1 word) _____, that ye may prove what is that good and acceptable and perfect (1 word) _____ of God.

8. I Pet.1:13 Wherefore gird up the loins of your mind. Be sober, and hope to the end for the (1 word) _____ that is to be brought to you at the (revealing) of (2 words) _____

9. Eph.4:22-23 …Put off concerning the former conversation the (2 words) _____, which is (1 word) _____ according to the deceitful lusts, and be (1 word) _____ in the spirit of your mind.

THE HEART:

10. Heb 10:22 Let us draw near (to God) with a (2 words) _____ in full assurance of faith, having our (1 word) _____ sprinkled from an evil conscience and our bodies washed with pure water. (ie, the Word)

11. 2 Cor.1:21-22 He which establisheth us with you in Christ and has anointed us is (1 word) _____, who hath also sealed us and given (us) the earnest of (2 words) _____ (of Christ) in our hearts. (When a Christian keeps the Spirit of Christ flowing in his heart most of the time, he is guaranteed not to fall away.)

THE SOUL:

12. Heb.10:39 But we are not of them who draw back unto (1 word) _____, but of them that believe to the saving of the (1 word) _____. (Saving of the soul is an ongoing process of renewing the mind and purifying the heart.)

13. 3 John 2 Beloved, I wish above all things that thou mayest (1 word) _____ and be in health, even as thy (1 word) _____ prospereth.

<u>A CHRISTIAN'S SPIRIT ROOM:</u> The Spirit of God dwells in a Christian's

new spirit from the moment he was born again.

Section Five
THE CHRISTIAN'S SOUL ROOM:

God will send the Spirit of Christ into your soul room as often as you prepare it for His entry.

14. Rev.3:20 Jesus said: Behold, I stand at the door and (1 word) _____ _____. If any man hear My voice and open the (1 word) _____, I will come (1 word)_____ to him and sup with him and he with Me. (Jesus spoke these words to the church – born-again Christians. The Spirit of Christ wants to spend more time in your heart/mind/soul room.)

There is a doorway between your spirit room and your soul room:

15. John 10:2 He that entereth in by the (1 word) _____ (the Spirit of Christ) is the (1 word)_____ of the flock.

16. John 10:3 To Him the porter openeth and the sheep (you and I) hear His (1 word) _____: and He calleth His own sheep by name and (2 word) _____out. (The Spirit of Christ desires to speak to you and lead you in all your ways.)

Section Six
THE DOORWAY BETWEEN THE CHRISTIAN'S SPIRIT AND SOUL:

God desires to see your doorway open at all times:

17. Eph.3:14 For this cause I (1 word)_____ my knees unto the (1 word) _____ of our Lord Jesus Christ.

18. Eph.3:16 That He would grant you, according to the riches of His glory, to be (1 word) _____ with might by His (Christ's) Spirit in the (2 words) _____

19. Eph.3:17 That (1 word) _____ (the Spirit of Christ) may dwell in your hearts by (1 word) _____: that ye, being rooted and grounded in love...

20. Eph.3:18-19 … may be able to comprehend with all saints what is the … love of Christ which passeth (1 word) _____, that ye might be filled with all the (1 word) _____ of God. (You are filled with the fullness of God when you have the Spirit of God in your born-again spirit, the Spirit of Christ in your heart/mind/soul, and the Holy Spirit in and around you.)

21. 2 Cor.5:17 Therefore, if any man be in Christ, he is a (2 words) _____ _____. …

Section Seven
WHY SHOULD I KEEP THE SPIRIT OF CHRIST IN MY SOUL ROOM AS OFTEN AS POSSIBLE?

22. John 15:4 Jesus said: Abide in (1 word) _____ and I in you (your soul room). As the branch (you) cannot (2 words) _____ of itself except it abide in the vine, no more can ye, except ye (3 words) _____ _____. (ie, abide in the Spirit of Christ.)

23. John 15:6 If a man abide not in (1 word) _____, he is cast out as a branch and is (1 word) _____. … (When your heart has become soiled, the Spirit of Christ must vacate the soul room. When that happens, your soul becomes estranged and it begins to wither.)

Section Eight
THE OLD TABERNACLE VERSUS THE NEW:

No one except the high priest could approach God in the Old Testament tabernacle, and that happened only once a year. The Spirit of God lives in every born-again Christian. We can approach God at any time – night or day. He is always there. Our job is to commune with Him. When we do, we cleanse the soul room so that the Spirit of Christ can flow in, and then out to others, like "rivers of living water".

ACCELERATED REVIEW SECTION – LESSON 14

Test your Bible maturity by doing the following. Return to:

1. **Sections I through 8 and** Summarize or outline the information under each.
2. **Summarize the overall statement made by this lesson.**

LESSON FIFTEEN
GOD'S HIGHER PLAN REQUIRES
TWO OCCUPIED ROOMS -- II

INTRODUCTION: If you are a Christian, you are the living, breathing temple of God today. The Spirit of God dwells in every born-again Christian. The Spirit of Christ will dwell in every Christian's soul if he sanctifies the area by speaking sincere words to God. As soon as a person is born again, he is righteous in his spirit room. His goal should be to be righteous in his soul room as regularly as possible.

Section One
PAUL CALLED THIS PROCESS "THE FELLOWSHIP MYSTERY":

1. Eph.3:8-9 (Paul said): … To me is this grace given that I should (1 word) _____ among the Gentiles the unsearchable riches of Christ, and to make all men see what is the (1 word) _____ of the mystery which from the beginning of the world hath been hid in God … . (Here, Paul referred to the two rooms and their purpose within the Christian.)

2. Eph.6:12 For we wrestle not against (1 word) _____ and blood, but against principalities and powers, and against the (4 words) _____ _____ of this world … . (The Spirit of God and the Spirit of Christ are in a Christian for the purpose of helping him overcome Satan and his demons on a moment-by-moment basis.)

Section Two
THE SPIRIT OF CHRIST WILL SPEAK TO YOU
WHEN YOU ACCEPT SATAN'S TEMPTATIONS:

3. Heb.12:6 Whom the Lord loves, He (1 word) _____ … . (God speaks to the Christian's conscience.)

4. Heb.12:11 Now no (1 word) _____ for the present seemeth to be joyous ... nevertheless, afterward it yieldeth the peaceable (3 words) _____ unto them which are exercised thereby.

Section Three

HIS CHASTENING IS TO REMIND US TO ALWAYS:
5. Heb.12:14 Follow (1 word) _____ with all men, and (1 word) _____, without which no man shall see the Lord.

Section Four
WHEN HE POINTS OUT A SIN, DO THE FOLLOWING:
6. I John 1:9 If we confess our (1 word) _____, He is (1 word) _____ and just to forgive us our sins and to (1 word) _____ us from all unrighteousness.

7. Eph.5:20 Giving (1 word) _____ always for all things unto God and the Father in the (1 word) _____ of our Lord Jesus Christ.

8. Rom.12:14 (1 word) _____ them which persecute you; bless and curse not.

9. I Cor.4:12-13 … Being reviled, we (1 word) _____; being persecuted, we suffer it (patiently). Being defamed, we (1 word) _____ ...

Section Five
THE SPIRIT OF CHRIST'S RELATIONSHIP TO THE CHURCH – US:
Answer the following questions:
10. Eph.5:23 Christ is _____
He is _____

11. Eph.5:25 Christ also _____
And He _____

12. Eph.5:26 to _____
With the _____

13. Eph.5:27 that He might present her to Himself a glorious _____ holy and without _____

14. Eph.5:29 Christ (3 words) _____ the church. (ie, Us)

ACCELERATED REVIEW SECTION – LESSON 15

Test your Bible maturity by doing the following. Return to:

1. **Sections I through 5 and** Summarize or outline the information under each.

2. **Summarize the overall statement made by this lesson.**

LESSON SIXTEEN
HOW TO KEEP YOUR SOUL ROOM OCCUPIED FOR LONGER PERIODS OF TIME

INTRODUCTION: Jesus said in Mt.5:48: "Be perfect as your Father in heaven is perfect." Jesus understands that we cannot live a life of perfection; but we can make it our goal to remain perfect for longer periods of time as we mature as Christians. Be wary of ever considering yourself perfect! This will immediately cause you to be guilty of the sin of pride.

Section One
THE FIRST STEP IN PERFECTION IS BEING BORN AGAIN:

1. John 17:23 Jesus spoke the following to His heavenly Father: I (2 words) _____, and Thou in Me; (why?) that they may be (2 words) _____ in one. … (The Father and the Son can be in a person only after he has been born again.)

Section Two
ONLY CHRIST HIMSELF CAN BE PERFECT ON-GOING:

2. I John 1:8 If we say that we have no sin, we (1 word) _____ ourselves, and the (1 word) _____ is not in us.

Section Three
HOW TO BECOME PERFECT FOR LONGER PERIODS:

3. Rom.12:2 Be not conformed to this (1 word) _____, but be ye transformed by the renewing of your (1 word) _____, that ye may prove what is that good and acceptable and perfect (3 words) _____ _____. (ie, When your heart is being perfect, you will hear from the Father, do what He asks, and prove out His plan for the moment.)

4. Gal.3:3 Are you so foolish? Having begun in the Spirit, are you now being made perfect by the (1 word) _____? (You cannot become perfect, even for a moment, by trying to do the do's and quit doing the don'ts. You become perfect only as you purge your heart/mind/soul by speaking words which cause the heart to be cleansed.)

5. 2 Tim.3:16-17 (Spend time in the Word because) all Scripture is given by (1 word) _____ of God, and is profitable for doctrine, for (1 word) _____, for (1 word) _____, and for instruction in (1 word) _____

6. James 3:2 (Bridle your tongue to say only God-accepted words, for we all stumble in many things.) If any man offend not in word, the same is a (2 words) _____ and able to bridle the (2 words) _____ _____ (with God's help).

7. 2 Cor.7:1 (Let us learn God's promises and realize they can be ours and) let us cleanse ourselves from all filthiness of the (3 words) _____ _____, perfecting holiness in the (3 words) _____ _____. (Again, this can be done only as you ask God's help in overcoming sin habits.)

8. 2 Cor.13:11 Become complete by being of … one (1 word) _____ (with fellow-believers) and by living in (1 word) _____. If you do these things, the God of love and (1 word) _____ will be with you.

9. Heb.12:25, 28 See that you (1 word) _____ not Him that speaketh to you. … Let us have grace whereby we may (3 words) _____ _____ with reverence and godly fear.

10. Heb.13:21 May God make you (1 word) _____ in every good work to do (works spoken to you by the Father).

11. Col.3:14-15 Above all these things, put on (1 word) _____ which is the bond of perfectness, and let the peace of God (1 word) _____ in your hearts, … and (3 words) _____

12. James 1:4 Let (1 word) _____ have her perfect work, that ye may be (3 words) _____, lacking nothing.

ACCELERATED REVIEW SECTION – LESSON 16

Test your Bible maturity by doing the following. Return to:

1. **Sections I through 3 and** Summarize or outline the information under each.
2. **Summarize the overall statement made by this lesson.**

LESSON SEVENTEEN
GOD'S HIGHER PLAN REQUIRES
FAITH - AND ACTING ON YOUR FAITH

INTRODUCTION: Paul tells us throughout His writings that faith is what pleases God – not works. James says that "faith without works is dead". So – to be a "Higher Plan" Christian, you must have faith and step out on your faith the instant He tells you to do so.

Section One
SCRIPTURE FROM PAUL AND JAMES:

1. Eph.2:8-9 (Paul wrote): By grace ye are saved by (1 word) _____ and that not of yourselves; it is the (1 word) _____ of God, not of (1 word) _____, lest any man should boast.

2. James 2:19-20 (James wrote): Thou believest there is one God. Thou doest well. The devils (1 word) _____ and also tremble! But wilt thou know, ... that faith without works is (1 word) _____?

Section Two

3. Rom.10:9 If thou shalt (1 word) _____ with thy mouth the Lord Jesus and shalt (1 word) _____ in thine heart that God hath (2 words) _____ from the dead, thou shalt be saved. (ie, To believe is to have <u>faith</u>. To confess with your mouth is the necessary <u>work</u>.)

Section Three
JAMES OFFERS AN EXAMPLE OF FAITH <u>WITH</u> WORKS:

4. James 2:21-22 James wrote: Was not Abraham our father justified by (1 word) _____ when he had offered Isaac his son on the altar? Do you see that (1 word) _____ was working together with his (1 word) _____, and by works, faith was made (1 word) _____?

5. James 2:26 James concludes: For as the body without the spirit is dead, so (3 words) _____ is dead also.

Section Four

A CLOSER LOOK AT JAMES' EXAMPLE:

<u>Abraham received His directions from God:</u>
6. Gen.22:1-2 And it came to pass after these things, that God (tested) Abraham and said unto him.... "Take now thy son, thine (2 words) _____ _____ Isaac, whom thou lovest, and get thee into the land of Moriah, and (2 words) _____ there for a burnt offering. ... (ie, Abraham received his instructions from the mouth of God. We should do likewise.)

<u>Abraham obeyed exactly how, when, and where God directed:</u>
7. Gen.22:3(&4) And Abraham rose up early in the morning and saddled his (donkey), and took two of his young men with him, (as well as) Isaac his son. And he (split) the wood for the burnt offering, and rose up and (4 words) _____ _____ of which God had told him.

<u>Abraham spoke his faith before witnesses:</u>
8. Gen.22:5(&6) Abraham said unto his young men, "Abide ye here with the (donkey); I and the lad will go yonder and worship, and we shall (2 words) __ _____ unto you."

<u>Abraham continued believing and speaking in faith:</u>
9. Gen.22:7-8 Isaac spake unto Abraham, his father, and he said, ... "Behold, the fire and the wood, but where is the (1 word) _____ for a burnt offering? And Abraham said, "My son, God will (1 word) _____ Himself a lamb for a burnt offer." So they went both of them together.

<u>Abraham believed God would raise Isaac from the dead if necessary:</u>
10. Gen.22:9(&10) They came to the place of which (5 words) _____ _____; and Abraham built an altar there and laid the wood in order; and bound Isaac his son and (5 words) _____ _____, upon the wood.

<u>God will always come through when you obey Him:</u>
11. Gen.22:11-12 The Angel of the Lord called unto ... Abraham. ... and said,

"Lay not thine hand upon the lad, neither do thou anything unto him; for now I know that thou (2 words) _____, seeing thou hast not (1 word) _____ thy ... only son from Me.

12. Gen.22:13   Abraham (2 words) _____ his eyes, and ... behind him (was) a ram caught in a thicket... Abraham went and took the ram, and (3 words) _____ for a burnt offering (instead) of his son.

God will reward those who obey His voice:
13. Gen.22:18   (God said to Abraham): In thy seed all the nations of the earth (shall) (2 words) _____, because thou hast obeyed My (1 word) _____. (We are recipients of Abraham's blessings when we obey God's voice.)

<u>**Section Five**</u>
GOD PROVIDES HIS VOICE TODAY – AND MORE:
God provides His written Word to instruct us:
14. 2 Tim.3:16   All Scripture is given by (3 words) _____ _____, and is profitable for (1 word) _____, for reproof, for correction, for instruction in (1 word) _____

God provides the five-fold ministry to teach us:
15. Eph.4:11   And (Jesus Himself) gave some (to be) apostles, and some prophets, and some evangelists, and some (3 words) _____ _____, for the perfecting of the saints, for the work of the ministry, for the edifying of the body of Christ. (us)

ACCELERATED REVIEW SECTION – LESSON 17

Test your Bible maturity by doing the following. Return to:
1. **Sections I through 5 and** Summarize or outline the information under each.
2. **Summarize the overall statement made by this lesson.**

_____

_____

LESSON EIGHTEEN
GOD'S HIGHER PLAN REQUIRES THAT YOU KNOW THE PROMISES – AND REFUSE TO FEAR

INTRODUCTION: Fear is the opposite of faith. Fear is sin. What does the Bible tell us about fear?

Section One
YOU MUST NOT FEAR BECAUSE . . .

Fear is the opposite of love:

1. I John 4:18 There is no fear in (1 word) _____, but perfect love (1 word) _____ out fear; because fear hath torment. He that feareth is not made (1 word) _____ in love.

2. I John 4:16 … God is love, and he that dwelleth in love dwelleth in God, and (3 words) _____. (The Spirit of Christ cannot remain in your soul room if love is not abiding there.)

Section Two
YOU MUST NOT FEAR BECAUSE . . .

Fear is disobedience to the Word:

3. Prov.3:25-26 (God's Word says): Be not (1 word) _____ of sudden fear, neither of the desolation of the wicked when it cometh. For the Lord shall be thy (1 word) _____, and He will keep your foot from being taken.

4. Rom.8:15 Ye have not received the (3 words) _____ again to fear, but ye have received the Spirit of adoption whereby we cry, "Abba, Father."

5. Psa.91:5-6 Thou (2 words) _____ be afraid for the terror by night, nor for the arrow that flieth by day, nor for the pestilence that walketh in darkness, nor for the destruction that wasteth at noonday.

Section Three
EXPECT TO BE FEARLESS IN EVERY SITUATION BECAUSE . . .

<u>You have God's promises to stand on:</u>

6. Psa.91:7   A thousand shall (1 word) _____ at thy your side, and ten thousand at thy right hand; but it shall not come nigh thee.

7. Psa.91:10   There shall no evil befall thee, neither shall any (1 word) _____ _____ come nigh thy dwelling.

8. Psa.91:4   (Expect God to) (2 words) _____ with His feathers, and under His wings shalt thou (1 word) _____; His (1 word) _____ shall be thy shield and buckler.

9. Isa.54:14   (Because) in (1 word) _____ shalt thou be (1 word) _____; thou shalt be far from oppression, for thou shalt not fear. ...

10. Psa.91:9   Because thou hast made the Lord ... thy (1 word) _____

Section Four
IN FACT – EXPECT TO BE HIGHLY COURAGEOUS BECAUSE . . .
<u>God Himself is your protector:</u>
11. Isa.43:2   When thou passest through the waters, (God) will be (2 words) _____. And through the rivers, they shall not overflow thee. When thou walkest through the fire, thou shall not be (1 word) _____ _____, neither shall the flame kindle upon thee.

12. Isa.41:10   So...Fear thou not; for (4 words) _____ _____; Be not dismayed, for I am thy God. I will (1 word) _____ thee; Yea, I will help thee, I will (1 word) _____ thee with the right hand of My righteousness. (ie, Jesus Christ.)

13. Rom.8:38-39   For I am persuaded that neither death nor life, nor angels, nor principalities, nor powers, nor things present nor things to come, nor height nor depth, nor any other creature, shall be able to (2 words) _____ _____ from the love of God which is in Christ Jesus our Lord. (Principalities and powers are the demonic realm.)

ACCELERATED REVIEW SECTION – LESSON 18

Test your Bible maturity by doing the following. Return to:

1. **Sections I through 4 and** Summarize or outline the information under each.
2. **Summarize the overall statement made by this lesson.**

LESSON NINETEEN
GOD'S HIGHER PLAN REQUIRES THAT YOU KNOW YOUR ARMOR

INTRODUCTION: Your enemy is looking for your weak point. He knows exactly what vulnerabilities you have, so do not give him an entry into your life. When the name of Jesus is spoken audibly, Satan knows he is a defeated foe.

Section One
SATAN IS YOUR ENEMY – MAN IS NOT!

1. Matt.5: 44 Jesus said: Love your enemies, (1 word) _____ them that (1 word) _____ you, (2 words) _____ to them that (2 words) _____, and (2 words)_____ them which spitefully use you and (2 words) _____

2. Eph.6:12 Paul said: For we do not (2 words) _____ flesh and blood, but against (1 word) _____, against (word)_____ _____, against the (3 words) _____of this age, against spiritual hosts of (5 words) _____

3. Eph.6:17 So…take the (3 words) _____, and the (4 words)_____which is the Word of God. (ie, Keep your mind full of the Word and stayed on Jesus Christ. Then, when Satan either whispers his lies or attacks you, speak the Word and the name of Jesus. He will cower if you truly know the power in that name.)

Section Two
YOUR ENEMY IS SATAN WHO HAS MANY NAMES, INCLUDING THE FOLLOWING:

Write the name(s) given to Satan in each verse:

4. I Pet.5:8 (2 names) _____

5. Matt.12:24 (2 names) _____

6. Isa.14:12 (2 names) _____

7. Eph.2:2 (2 names) _____

8. Rev.9:11 (3 names) _____
_____

9. Rev.12:9 (4 names) _____
_____

10. Rev.20:2 (4 names)_____
_____

11. John 8:44 (4 names)_____
_____

12. 2 Cor.4:4 (1 name) _____

13. Rev.12:10 (1 name) _____

14. Ezek.28:14 (1 name) _____ (This was his name before he was cast down.)

Section Three
WEAR YOUR DEFENSIVE ARMOR AROUND THE CLOCK:
Name the armor which covers each area listed below:

15. Eph..6:14 Around your waist (as your holster) you must wear what? (4 words) _____. ... ("Truth" is knowledge and wisdom coming straight from heaven. You can be most effective against Satan when you are following the Holy Spirit's leading.)

16. Eph.6:14 ... Over your chest area (as a breastplate) you must wear what? (4 words) _____. (A proper breastplate will cover both your spirit and your soul. A person who has the Spirit of God in his born-again spirit and the Spirit of Christ flowing through his heart/mind/soul has on his breastplate of righteousness.)

17. Eph.6:15 What armor must you put on your feet? (6 words) _____. (The gospel of Jesus Christ is a gospel of peace. Additionally, the Word teaches how to walk in peace every day. This, too, is the gospel of peace.)

18. Eph.6:17a What armor must you use to cover your head (ie, mind)? (4 words) _____. (Have your mind renewed daily by the Word. Be confident of your salvation and the faithfulness of God when you call on Him.)

19. Eph.6:16 Over your full suit of armor you must carry a shield which is called what? (4 words) _____. (When you have put on all the afore-stated, take up a strong shield of faith, trusting in the power and authority which is in the spoken name of Jesus.)

Section Four
CARRY YOUR OFFENSIVE WEAPON AROUND THE CLOCK:

20. Eph.6:17b What weapon must you use with great confidence? (11 words) _____. (When Satan hovers, quote or paraphrase a verse from the Word of God and speak it with confidence, using the powerful name of Jesus.)

Section Five
SPEAKING THE NAME OF JESUS HAS
GREAT POWER OVER SATAN BECAUSE....

21. Col.2:15 …Jesus spent three days in Hades conquering Satan (when everyone thought He was lying dead in a tomb). While He was in Hades, He disarmed (1 word) _____ and (1 word) _____ (demons) and made a (2 words) _____ of them (3 words) _____ in it.

22. I John 3:8b Jesus came to earth in human form to destroy (5 words) _____ _____

Complete this sentence:

23. I John 4:4b When you use the name of Jesus, Satan has to flee, because (14 words) _____

Section Six
SATAN RECEIVED HIS POWER BY DECEIVING EVE:

24. Gen.1:26 Satan wrested away the power which God had given Adam and Eve when He said: "Let us make man in Our image and let them have (1 word) _____."

25. Gen.2:16-17 (God told His first couple): Of every tree of the garden thou mayest (2 words) _____; but of the tree of the (1 word) _____ of good and evil thou shalt not eat, for in the day thou eatest thereof, thou shalt surely (1 word) _____

26. Gen.3:6 (But after Satan came to Eve and enticed her), she took of the fruit thereof and did eat. She also gave it to her husband, and … he (2 word) _____. (At that moment, all of the dominion over the earth which God had given to Adam and Eve was given over to Satan's hand. He has had it ever since – except when we retake it using the name of Jesus.)

ACCELERATED REVIEW SECTION – LESSON 19

Test your Bible maturity by doing the following. Return to:
1. **Sections I through 6 and** Summarize or outline the information under each.
2. **Summarize the overall statement made by this lesson.**

LESSON TWENTY
GOD'S HIGHER PLAN INVOLVES THREE STAGES OF SALVATION

INTRODUCTION: Christians speak of the new birth as "being saved" but that term is not entirely accurate. The new birth produces a new spirit in which the Spirit of God dwells. It requires only a moment to appropriate. You then have the remainder of your life on earth to accomplish the saving of the soul. A person can be confident of his eternal life once he has been born again, but additional great and glorious promises come with the life-long process of renewing the mind.

Section One
THE NEW BIRTH -- REGENERATION -- THE FIRST "SALVATION":

<u>Is a gift you receive when you believe and speak:</u>
1. Rom.10:9-10 If thou shalt (1 word) _____ with thy mouth the Lord Jesus and shalt (1 word) _____ in thine heart that God hath (2 words) _____ from the dead, thou shalt be saved. For with the heart man believeth unto (1 word) _____ (of the soul), and with the mouth confession is made unto salvation. (The heart of a Christian is purged by the words of his mouth.)

<u>It is not a visible birth:</u>
2. John 3:3, 8 (Jesus said): ... Except a man be (2 words) _____ _____, he cannot see the kingdom of God. ... The wind bloweth where it listeth, and thou hearest the sound thereof, but canst not tell whence it cometh and whither it goeth; So is everyone that is (4 words) _____ _____. (Just as the physical ear can hear the invisible wind, those around the new Christian will hear something new in him. He will speak differently as he tells of his new birth with joy.)

.
<u>Is eternal unless you renounce Him:</u>
3. John 3:18 He who believeth on (Jesus) is not (1 word) _____ but he that believeth not is condemned already because he has not believed in the name of the only begotten (3 words) _____

4. John 3:16 For God so (1 word) _____ the world that He gave His only begotten Son, that whosoever believeth in (1 word) _____ should not perish but have (1 word) _____ life.

This first stage of salvation makes it possible (but not inevitable) to live an abundant, overcoming, and emotionally healthy life. It breaks the Father's heart that many Christians fail to move into the second stage of salvation – the renewing of the mind.

Section Two
RENEWING OF THE MIND –THE SECOND "SALVATION":

Call on the name of the Lord regularly throughout the day:

5. Psa.91:15-16 (God says through the words of David): He shall call upon Me, and I will (2 words) _____. I will be with him in trouble. I will (1 word) _____ him and (1 word) _____ him. With long life will I satisfy him, and shew him My (1 word) _____ (of the soul).

Ask for God's help in subduing old habits:

6. Rom.12:1 (As Paul said): I beseech you, … by the mercies of God, that ye (3 words) _____ a living sacrifice, holy, acceptable unto God, which is your reasonable service.

7. Rom.6:19 … As ye have yielded your members servants to uncleanness, and to (1 word) _____, … even so now yield your members servants to (1 word) _____ unto holiness.

Study the Word until you take on the attributes of Jesus Christ – The Word of God:

8. 2 Cor.3:18 We … beholding as in a glass the glory of the Lord, (through the Word) are (being) (1 word) _____ into the same image from glory to glory, even as by the (1 word) _____ of the Lord.

9. Eph.4:21-23 If so be ye have (1 word) _____ Him (the Word and His voice) and have been taught by Him … (you will be putting)… off the old man … and you will be (1 word) _____ in the spirit of your mind.

<u>Expect life's circumstances to mold you into Christ's image -- if you praise Him:</u>

10. Rom.8:28-29   We know that (2 words) _____ work together for good to them that love God, to them who are the called according to His purpose. For whom He did foreknow, He also did predestinate to be (1 word) _____ to the image of His Son. ... (God's plan paved the way for every believer to move to the higher level, but not all will. Will you?

Section Three
RECEIVING A GLORIFIED BODY – THE THIRD "SALVATION":

11. Phil.3:14 Paul said: I (1 word) _____ toward the mark for the prize of the (2 words) _____ of God in Christ Jesus. (ie, I press toward the higher level.)

12. Phil.3:20-21 For our conversation is (already) in (1 word) _____, from whence also we look for the Savior, the Lord Jesus Christ, who will change our vile (1 word) _____ that it may be fashioned like unto His glorious body. (This is speaking of the glorified body which will be ours at the rapture and resurrection.)

Receiving a glorified body will complete our third stage of salvation. Praise God!

ACCELERATED REVIEW SECTION – LESSON 20

Test your Bible maturity by doing the following. Return to:
1. **Sections I through 3 and** Summarize or outline the information under each.
2. **Summarize the overall statement made by this lesson.**

_____
_____
_____
_____
_____
_____
_____

The following Bible study workbooks are also available:
Are You Equipped For the Work?
Believe To Receive! & Speak Or Leak!
Bible Study Made Fun!
God Looks On the Heart
Know the Fullness of "Christ"
Life Lessons From the Bible
Line Upon Line – Precept Upon Precept
Luke: The New Birth and Baby Christianity
The Rapture! Then What?
Understand the Bible Today!
Whet Your Bible Appetite!
Especially For Youth! Book One
Especially For Youth! Book Two
Especially For Youth! Book Three
Especially For Youth! Book Four
Teacher's Manual! – Especially For Youth!

OVERVIEW

OUTLINE

LESSON 1 – EVIDENCE THAT GOD REQUIRES SHED BLOOD:
INTRODUCTION: Throughout the Old Testament, God was teaching His people to look forward to the day His Son would shed His own perfect blood.
1. God was pleased with Abel's blood sacrifice.
2. God had Israel place lamb's blood for protection from death.
3. Jesus placed His own shed blood on the mercy seat in heaven to satisfy God.
4. Jesus' blood continues to save new Christians today.
5. Jesus' blood clears the way for us to enter into the very presence of God.
6. Jesus' blood will save us from the final wrath.
7. Jesus' blood purchases our right to forgiveness throughout our lives.
8. Jesus' blood makes us as though we had never sinned.

LESSON 2 – BUT WE MUST CONTINUE TO BELIEVE:
INTRODUCTION: The Bible makes it very clear that you can be truly born again, then decide to renounce Jesus Christ at a later time. But you can also be positive that God will never renounce you unless you first renounce His Son.
1. There are three differing doctrines about eternal life.
2. The correct doctrine is – You Can Be Sure!
3. God will never reject you unless you renounce Him fully and completely.
4. This lesson lists the things a Christian should do to continue "continuing".

LESSON 3 – GOD PLEADS WITH US TO GO ON TO MATURITY:
INTRODUCTION: The carnal mind is diametrically opposite to the mind which follows God's leading. The carnal mind wavers between following self-thinking and Satan's darts.
1. A carnal Christian is an immature Christian.
2. Carnality results from spending little time in the Word.
3. Carnality produces luke-warmness.
4. Carnality results in non-tithing.
5. Carnality is evidenced by a carnal mouth and a carnal heart.
6. This lesson teaches how one can turn from carnality.

LESSON 4 – MATURITY BEGINS WITH OVERCOMING SATAN:

INTRODUCTION: God has promised to avenge us on human enemies, but we alone are responsible for dealing with Satan. We must command the devil to do what we demand, always using the name of Jesus.

1. We must pray for all to learn how to deal with Satan.
2. We must choose to defeat Satan whenever he raises his ugly head.
3. We defeat Satan by walking according to God's quiet voice.
4. We defeat Satan by commanding him to leave in the name of Jesus.

LESSON 5 – MATURITY REQUIRES *AGAPE* LOVE:

INTRODUCTION: The New Testament was written in the Greek language which has greater specificity in some of its words. For example, the Greek differentiates among the following words for "Love". (1) *Agape* love is the God-kind of love which flows from the Spirit of God within a Christian under the right conditions. (2) Brotherly love is love which flows from the soul.

1. Jesus commanded *agape* love.
2. Only God can produce *agape* love.
3. I must prepare my soul to receive *agape* love by speaking Godly words.
4. I must be consistently walking in brotherly love.
5. I must consistently speak blessings on any who mistreat me, and thank God.
6. I must walk in the light which He gives me.

LESSON 6 – MATURITY REQUIRES CHURCH ATTENDANCE:

INTRODUCTION: Televised messages have their place for shut-ins; but God intended that His body, the church, meet together and minister to one another as the various parts of a human body take care of the other parts.

1. Regular church attendance is needed because we need one another.
2. We most often practice our ministry gifts with our church family.
3. So begin being faithful today.

LESSON 7 – MATURITY REQUIRES PRAYER:

INTRODUCTION: Pray when you are at home; pray when you go out. Pray

when things look good; pray when things look bad. Paul says in I Thes.5:17 that we should pray without ceasing. Prayer takes many forms as evidenced below:
1. Prayer must include praises and thanksgivings.
2. Tell God what you need, and then express thanks that it is on its way.
3. Intercede for the needs of others.
4. Give thanks for the good and the bad, even though He doesn't send the bad.
5. Speak in line with your prayers, or else you override them.

LESSON 8 – MATURITY REQUIRES PATIENT SUFFERING:
INTRODUCTION: Patience is a virtue highly esteemed by our Father. This is a study of patient suffering.
1. God is our example of patient suffering.
2. God asks us to suffer patiently.
3. Faith is necessary to accomplish patient suffering.

LESSON 9 – MATURITY REQUIRES 2 KINDS OF RIGHTEOUSNESS:
INTRODUCTION: Why does God require shed blood and belief in Jesus Christ for all, yet He has a Higher Plan which all Christians should press toward? The answers to that question is that God has two kinds of righteousness. The first kind of righteousness is the "Righteousness of God". The second kind of righteousness is the "Righteousness of Christ". This is a study of the two, their meanings, and their rewards.
1. The "Righteousness of God" is the new birth.
2. Explanation of the new birth process.
3. Details about the new birth righteousness.
4. The "Righteousness of God" remains in man's spirit without leaving (unless he renounces Christ.)
5. The "Righteousness of Christ" is the renewing mind.
6. Details about the renewing mind.
7. The "Righteousness of Christ" was possible during Old Testament times.

LESSON 10 – MATURITY REQUIRES A SHINING SOUL:

INTRODUCTION: If you are a Christian, you are a lighthouse. Is your light shining bright? Can others find their way by keeping their eyes on you? The purpose of this lesson is to teach every Christian to become high voltage, bright lighthouses for those around them.

1. How one becomes a shining Christian.
2. How one continues shining for longer periods of time.

LESSON 11 – MATURITY REQUIRES HUMILITY:

INTRODUCTION: Nations, as well as individuals, must humble themselves before God.

1. God requires it of nations.
2. God requires it of maturing Christians.
3. God requires it of you.

LESSON 12 – MATURITY REQUIRES FORGIVENESS:

INTRODUCTION: A pure heart is a heart which rests in peace and goodwill toward God and others. God desires that every Christian walk in peace.

1. Forgiveness of others is necessary for a peaceful environment.
2. It is necessary to keep peace between individuals.
3. It is a prerequisite for maturing.
4. It is a prerequisite for peace.
5. Jesus commanded it.
6. Jesus taught how to resolve legal conflicts between Christians.
7. More teachings on resolving conflicts.
8. To accomplish true forgiveness of others, audibly speak blessings on them.
9. God's forgiveness of us is necessary also. The Word tells us how to get it.

LESSON 13 – MATURITY REQUIRES TITHING:

INTRODUCTION: Are you financially strapped? God's Word has the answer to every solution. He desires to see His children prosper, and his Word tell us how.

1. Tithing is a prerequisite to overall prosperity.
2. It requires prayer and commitment.
3. Faithful tithing comes from knowing the Word.
4. It requires a heart of thanksgiving.
5. It is good for the soul.
6. It is over and above giving to the needs of others.
7. It requires that you set priorities.

LESSON 14 – MATURITY REQUIRES TWO OCCUPIED ROOMS:
INTRODUCTION: If you are a Christian, you are the living, breathing temple of God. You are His three-part tabernacle on earth. You are spirit, soul, and body. Heaven's plan is: That the Spirit of God occupy your spirit room; that the Spirit of Christ occupy your soul room; and that you master your flesh with their help.
1. Picture of the Old Testament tabernacle.
2. Picture of the New Testament tabernacle.
3. Details about the spirit room.
4. Details about the soul room.
5. Christ in the soul room.
6. The doorway between the spirit and soul rooms.
7. The Spirit of Christ longs to abide in your soul room.
8. Today's tabernacle is superior to the old one.

LESSON 15 – TWO ROOMS, CONTINUED:
INTRODUCTION: If you are a Christian, you are the living, breathing temple of God today. The Spirit of God dwells in every born-again Christian. The Spirit of Christ will dwell in every Christian's soul if he sanctifies the area by speaking sincere words to God. As soon as a person is born again, he is righteous in his spirit room. His goal should be to be righteous in his soul room as regularly as possible.
1. The process of Christ moving into your prepared soul room is called "the fellowship mystery".
2. It includes chastening.

3. It includes reminding us to forgive.
4. It includes reminding us to confess our sins.
5. It includes making Christ our Head.

LESSON 16 – MATURITY REQUIRES AN ABIDING SPIRIT OF CHRIST:

INTRODUCTION: Jesus said in Matt.5:48: "Be perfect as your Father in heaven is perfect." Jesus understands that we cannot live a life of perfection; but we can make it our goal to remain perfect for longer periods of time as we mature as Christians. Be wary of ever considering yourself perfect! This will immediately cause you to be guilty of the sin of pride.

1. An abiding Spirit of Christ is possible in those who have been born again.
2. It requires recognizing that no one can be perfect 100% of the time.
3. It requires your knowing how to become progressively perfect.

LESSON 17 – MATURITY REQUIRES FAITH AND ACTING ON IT:

INTRODUCTION: Paul tells us throughout His writings that faith is what pleases God –not works. James says that "faith without works is dead". So – to be a "Higher Plan" Christian, you must have faith and step out on your faith the instant He tells you to.

1. Verses on the importance of faith.
2. Verses on Faith + Works = Real Faith.
3. Verses showing Abraham's example of Faith + Works.
4. Verses showing that God speaks to people today, just as He did to Abraham.

LESSON 18 – MATURITY REQUIRES KNOWING THE WORD AND REFUSING TO FEAR:

INTRODUCTION: Fear is the opposite of faith. Fear is sin. What does the Bible tell us about fear?

1. Why fear is displeasing to God.
2. More reasons why fear is displeasing to God.
3. Why you can expect to live without fear.

4. Why you can expect to be highly courageous.

LESSON 19 – MATURITY REQUIRES KNOWING YOUR ENEMY, YOUR ARMOR, AND YOUR WEAPONS:

INTRODUCTION: Your enemy is looking for your weak point. He knows exactly what vulnerabilities you have, so do not give him an entry into your life. When the name of Jesus is spoken audibly, Satan knows he is a defeated foe.
1. Satan, not man, is your enemy.
2. Satan is well-described by his many names.
3. Christians must wear protective armor against him.
4. They must carry a full arsenal of effective weapons.
5. They must speak the name of Jesus with authority when dealing with Satan.
6. Satan is a deceiver. Do not allow him to deceive you.

LESSON 20 – MATURITY REQUIRES PRESSING TOWARD THE SECOND AND THIRD SALVATION:

INTRODUCTION: Christians speak of the new birth as "being saved" but that term is not entirely accurate. The new birth produces a new spirit in which the Spirit of God dwells. It requires only a moment to appropriate. You then have the remainder of your life on earth to accomplish the saving of the soul. A person can be confident of his eternal life once he has been born again, but additional great and glorious promises come with the life-long process of renewing the mind.
1. Salvation of the spirit – the new birth.
2. Salvation of the soul – renewing of the soul/mind.
3. Receiving the glorified body -- in the resurrection or the rapture.

Van & Barbara Ballew can be contacted at Barbvan452@aol.com

Other Bible Study Workbooks By Van and Barbara Ballew are:
Are You Equipped For the Work?

Bible Study Made Fun!
God Looks On the Heart
Know the Fullness of "Christ"
Life Lessons From the Bible
Line Upon Line – Precept Upon Precept
Luke: The New Birth and Baby Christianity
The Rapture! Then What?
Understand the Bible Today!
Whet Your Bible Appetite!
Especially For Youth! (Books One through Four)

ANSWER SECTION

LESSON ONE
GOD REQUIRES SHED BLOOD

Each lesson in this workbook is entitled with a truth which every believer should know. The following verses prove the truth stated in this title.

<u>Throughout these lessons you will be asked to find the stated verse and fill in each blank. Please use the King James Version because it is the version most readily available to all:</u>

EVIDENCE ONE:

God taught Adam His requirement for a blood sacrifice. Adam and Eve had two sons. <u>God was pleased with Abel's blood sacrifice.</u> God was not pleased with Cain's sacrifice because it was not the blood sacrifice which He required. Cain was so jealous of Abel that he killed him.

<u>God said to Cain:</u>
1. Gen.4:10 What hast thou done? The voice of thy brother's blood ***CRIETH*** unto Me from the ***GROUND.***

EVIDENCE TWO:

The people of Israel were God's special people; however the pharaoh in Egypt made slaves of them. The pharaoh was cruel to the Jews and made impossible demands of them, so God designed a plan to rescue His people. He then used Moses and Aaron to warn Egypt that He would kill the first son of every family if they did not allow the Israelites to return to their homeland. Pharaoh refused to free the Israelites, so God had to keep His word. <u>To protect His special people from the curse, God said to spread lamb's blood.</u>

<u>God said to Moses:</u>
2. Ex.12:3 Speak ye unto all the congregation of ***ISRAEL***. ... They shall take to them every man a ***LAMB***, a lamb ... for a house(hold).

3, Ex.12:5-6 Your lamb shall be without ***BLEMISH*** (imperfection), a ***LAMB*** of the first year. ... Keep it up until the ***FOURTEENTH*** day, ... and the whole assembly ... shall kill it in the ***EVENING***.

4. Ex.12:7 And they shall take of the ***BLOOD*** and strike it on the ***TWO*** side posts and on the ***UPPER*** door post of the houses. ...

5. Ex.12:12 I (God) will pass through the land of ***EGYPT*** this night and will ***SMITE*** (kill) all the firstborn in the land of Egypt. ...

6. Ex.12:13 ...And when I see the ***BLOOD*** I will pass over you, and the ***PLAGUE*** (of death) shall not be upon ***YOU*** ...

7. Who is our Lamb without blemish? ***JESUS CHRIST***.

8. If animal blood protected Israel from the curse of death, Jesus' blood will protect us from the curse of punishment and death in eternal ***HELL***.

EVIDENCE THREE:

God's requirement for blood sacrifices continued from Adam up to the present time. <u>Jesus had to complete the process by putting His own shed blood on the mercy seat in heaven thereby winning us back from Satan.</u>

9. Heb.9:12 Neither by the blood of goats and calves, but by (Christ's) own blood, He entered in ***ONCE*** into (heaven's) holy place, having obtained ***ETERNAL*** redemption for ***US***. ("Redemption" is Christ's having won us back from the domain of Satan which began with Adam's fall.)

EVIDENCE FOUR:
God's requirement for blood sacrifices continues now. <u>The blood Jesus placed on the mercy seat in heaven continues to cleanse new Christians today.</u>
10. Heb.9:22 And almost all things are by the law purged (cleansed) with ***BLOOD***, and without shedding of blood is no ***REMISSION***. ("Remission" means complete removal. Without the shedding of Christ's blood there would be no complete removal of man's sin.)

EVIDENCE FIVE:
<u>Jesus' blood on the mercy seat in heaven provides the way for us to enter into the very presence of God.</u>
11. Heb.10:19-20 Having therefore, brethren, boldness to enter into the holiest by the blood of ***JESUS***, by a ***NEW*** and living way … through the veil, that is, … His ***FLESH***. … Heb.10:22 Let us draw near (to God) with a ***TRUE HEART*** in full assurance of ***FAITH***. …

EVIDENCE SIX:
<u>Jesus' blood on the mercy seat in heaven will save us from God's wrath when He dispenses the final punishment on the lost.</u>
12. Heb.10:28 He that despised Moses' law (including blood sacrifices) died without mercy under two or three ***WITNESSES.***

13. Heb.10:29 Of how much sorer punishment … shall he be thought worthy, who hath trodden under foot the ***SON OF GOD*** and hath counted the blood of the covenant an … ***UNHOLY*** thing. …

EVIDENCE SEVEN:
<u>Jesus' blood on the mercy seat in heaven purchases our continuing right to God's forgiveness of sins.</u>
14. Eph.1:7 In (Jesus Christ) we have ***REDEMPTION*** through His blood,

the forgiveness of ***SINS*** according to the riches of His ***GRACE***. ("Grace" is undeserved mercy and power. This is what we receive as a result of Jesus Christ's death on the cross.)

EVIDENCE EIGHT:
Jesus' blood on the mercy seat in heaven makes us as though we had never sinned. Because of Jesus, God casts our sins into the sea of forgetfulness.
15. Rom.5:8-9 God commendeth His love toward us, in that while we were yet ***SINNERS***, Christ ***DIED*** for us. ... Being now ***JUSTIFIED*** by His blood, we shall be ***SAVED FROM WRATH*** through Him. (God sent His Son to die for us while we were still lost. His shed blood made us just as if we'd never sinned. Consequently, we shall not be part of the wrath of God which will come on the lost.)

LESSON TWO
GOD REQUIRES THAT YOU CONTINUE BELIEVING IN JESUS CHRIST AND HIS BLOOD

INTRODUCTION: The Bible makes it very clear that you can be truly born again, then decide to renounce Jesus Christ at a later time. You can be positive that God will never renounce you unless you first renounce His Son.

Section One
ALL CHRISTIANS BELIEVE ONE OF THESE THREE DOCTRINES:
There are denominations which teach each of the following:

A. Once Saved, Always Saved: (ie, These believe that no real Christian would ever turn away.)

B. You Can Never Be Sure of Your Salvation: (ie, These believe that we are constantly adding and subtracting "points" which will earn, or lose, their eternal life.)

C. You Can Be Sure of Your Salvation--But You Can Choose To Renounce Christ: (This lesson seeks to prove from the Word of God that the third doctrine is the correct one.)

RECAP: All three cannot be correct. So, which one is the true doctrine?

Section Two
THESE VERSES VERIFY THAT A CHRISTIAN CAN BE SURE OF HIS ETERNAL SALVATION:

1. I John 5:13 (John wrote): These things have I written to you that **BELIEVE** in the name of the **SON OF GOD**, that ye may **KNOW** that ye have **ETERNAL LIFE**, and that ye may **BELIEVE** on the name of the Son of God.

2. Gal.3:1-2 (Paul wrote to those who felt they must continue through life earning their salvation. He said): O foolish Galatians! Who hath bewitched you that ye should not obey the **TRUTH**, before whose eyes Jesus Christ hath been evidently set forth as **CRUCIFIED** among you? ... Received ye the Spirit by the **WORKS** of the law, or by the **HEARING** of faith?

3. Gal.3:3 Are you so foolish? Having begun in the (born-again) **SPIRIT**, are you now (being) made perfect by the (works of the) **FLESH**?

4. Gal.4:9 ... (How is it that you) **TURN AGAIN** to the weak and beggarly elements, whereunto ye desire again to be in **BONDAGE**?

5. Gal.5:4 Christ is become of no effect unto you. Whosoever of you are justified by the law, ye are **FALLEN FROM GRACE**.

6. Gal.5:8 This persuasion cometh not from (God) who **CALLETH YOU**. (If not from God, then it must come from Satan.)

Section Three
GOD WILL NEVER REJECT YOU, BUT YOU CAN REJECT HIM AND HIS SON:

It is possible to be born again and later reject Jesus Christ and the Father:

7. Col.1:21-22 You that were sometimes alienated (lost), ..., yet (Jesus Christ)

hath now **RECONCILED** ... through (his death), to present you **HOLY** and unblameable, and unreproveable in **HIS** sight. (ie, You were once lost, but then you were born again.)

8. Col.1:23 (But you must) continue in the **FAITH**, grounded and settled, and be not *MOVED AWAY* from the hope of the **GOSPEL** which ... was preached to every creature ... under heaven. ... (You must choose to never audibly renounce the Father and the Son. Just as you were saved by audibly speaking your belief, you can be "unsaved" by audibly speaking your unbelief.)

9. Heb.2:1 Therefore we (must) give the more earnest heed to the things which **WE HAVE HEARD**, ... lest we let them slip away.

10. Heb.3:12 Take heed, brethren, lest there be in any of you an evil heart of **UNBELIEF**, (causing you to depart) from the **LIVING GOD**.

11. Heb.12:25 See that ye **REFUSE NOT** Him that **SPEAKETH** (to you inside your heart.) ...

Section Four
WHAT CAN WE DO TO PROTECT OURSELVES FROM EVER TURNING AWAY?

12. Heb.12:1 ... Let us *LAY ASIDE* every weight, and (put away) the **SIN** which doth so easily beset us, and let us run with **PATIENCE** the race that is set before us. (Ask God's help as you lay aside everything that draws you away from Jesus Christ and your church family.)

13. Heb.3:6 ... Hold fast the confidence and the **REJOICING** of the hope firm unto **THE END.** (Do not allow Satan to send his fiery darts into your thoughts. Rejoice audibly in your confidence in Jesus Christ, and your expectation of His return.)

14. Heb.3:13 Exhort one another daily, ... lest any of you be **HARDENED** through the deceitfulness of **SIN.**

15. Col.1:23-24 If ye **CONTINUE** in the faith, grounded and settled, and be

not ***MOVED*** away from the hope of the gospel which ye have heard ... I rejoice in my sufferings for you. ... (God's promise: Christians who remain in the Word of Truth will never, ever turn away.)

16. I John 2:24-25 Let that, therefore, ***ABIDE*** in you which ye have heard from the beginning. (If you do this), ye also shall continue in the ***SON*** and in the ***FATHER.*** And this is the promise that He hath promised us – even ***ETERNAL LIFE***.

17. I John 2:23 (The Bible warns us of other religions which refuse to acknowledge the Lordship of Jesus Christ. John says): "Whosoever ***DENIETH THE SON*** ... hath not the Father ..."

CONCLUSION: To qualify for eternal life, a person must:
- Believe that Jesus Christ is the Son of God.
- Believe that Jesus died on the cross and rose from the dead.
- Audibly confess the above beliefs.
- Continue to believe the above.
- Never audibly renounce Jesus Christ and His sacrifices.

TO QUALIFY FOR GOD'S <u>HIGHER</u> PLAN, A CHRISTIAN MUST DO THE FOLLOWING AS WELL:

LESSON THREE
GOD'S HIGHER PLAN REQUIRES "MATURE CHRISTIANS" – NOT "CARNAL CHRISTIANS"

INTRODUCTION: The carnal mind is diametrically opposite to the mind which follows God's leading. The carnal mind wavers between following self-thinking and Satan's darts.

Section One
WHAT IS THE CARNAL MIND?

1. Rom.8:7 The carnal mind is enmity (an enemy) against God; for it is not subject to the *LAW OF GOD*, (ie, following God's leading) neither indeed can be.

2. Rom.8:5 For they that are (living) after the *FLESH* do mind the things of the flesh, but they that are after the *SPIRIT* (set their minds on) the things of the Spirit.

3. Rom.8:6 (Beware because) to be carnally minded is *DEATH* but to be spir-itual minded is *LIFE AND PEACE.*

Section Two
A CARNAL MINDED CHRISTIAN HAS NOT SPENT TIME IN THE WORD:

Paul instructs these baby Christians:

4. Heb.5:12 When ... ye ought to be *TEACHERS* (by this time), ye have need that one teach you again ... the first *PRINCIPLES* of the oracles (wisdom) of God. And you are become such as have need of *MILK*, and not of strong meat. (ie, Some Christians never study the Word for themselves, always wanting someone else to feed them like babies. "Meat" means the deeper truths of God, such as you will be studying in these lessons. "Meat" also means hearing directly from God and obeying Him.)

5. Heb.6:1-2 Therefore, leaving the (baby) principles of the *DOCTRINE* of Christ, let us go on to *PERFECTION* (maturity). ... (Teachers should not repeatedly teach the same few things. God's Word always provides new truths.)

6. Heb.6:11 We desire that every one of you do shew the same *DILIGENCE* to the full assurance of hope unto the end.

Section Three
A CARNAL MINDED CHRISTIAN IS LUKEWARM, AT BEST:

7. Rev.3:15 (Jesus said to the church at Laodicea:) "I know thy works, that thou art neither *COLD NOR HOT*. ... (Neither for or against God.)

8. Rev.3:17-18 Because thou sayest, "I am *RICH* and ... have need of nothing," ... I counsel thee to buy of Me *GOLD* tried in the fire (a time of hardship that thou mayest be rich and ... clothed in) *WHITE* raiment.... (Jesus is telling the lukewarm Christian to use the tribulation period to earn his white robe of righteousness.)

Section Four
A CARNAL MINDED CHRISTIAN DOES NOT GIVE BACK WHAT IS RIGHTFULLY GOD'S:

9. Mal.3:8 Will a man *ROB* God? Yet ye have robbed Me ... in *TITHES* and *OFFERINGS.*

10. Mal.3:10-11 Bring ye all the tithes into the *STOREHOUSE* that there may be *MEAT* in Mine house, ... Prove Me now herewith, saith the Lord of hosts, if I will not open (for) you the *WINDOWS* of heaven. ... That there shall not be room enough to *RECEIVE* it. And I will rebuke the *DEVOURER* (Satan) for your sakes so that he will not destroy the *FRUITS* of your ground. ...

Section Five
A CARNAL CHRISTIAN HAS A CARNAL MOUTH AND A CARNAL HEART:

11. Eph.4:29-30 (The Word of God says): Let no corrupt communication proceed out of your *MOUTH,* but that which is good to the use of *EDIFYING*, (building up) that it may minister grace unto the hearers; and grieve not the *HOLY SPIRIT* of God. ...

12. Eph.4:31-32 Let all *BITTERNESS* and wrath, and *ANGER*, and

clamor, and evil ***SPEAKING*** be put away from you, with all ***MALICE*** (bad intentions.) And be ye kind one to another, tenderhearted and forgiving one another, even as God for Christ's sake hath forgiven ***YOU.***

13. Heb.12:14-15 Follow peace with all men, and holiness, without which no man shall see the ***LORD***, looking diligently lest … any root of ***BITTERNESS*** springing up trouble you, and thereby many be ***DEFILED***. (When division arises among Christians it affects the entire church; and some may even turn away because of it.)

Section Six
TURN FROM YOUR FORMER CARNALITY AND DO THIS:

14. Rom.12:1-2 …Present your bodies a living ***SACRIFICE*** holy and acceptable unto God, which is your reasonable ***SERVICE,*** and be not conformed to this world, but be ye transformed by the renewing of your ***MIND*** that ye may prove what is that good and acceptable and perfect ***WILL OF GOD***. (When you present your body and mind to do whatever God speaks to you, He will bring about His intended result. This will prove that He was the one who spoke to you and that He used you to accomplish His perfect plan.)

15. Col.3:2-3 Set your affection (desire) on things ***ABOVE***, not on things on the ***EARTH,*** for ye (your old man) is dead and your life is hid with ***CHRIST*** in God. (You need to seek the moment-by-moment help of God and the Spirit of Christ.)

LESSON FOUR
GOD'S HIGHER PLAN REQUIRES THAT CHRISTIANS TAKE AUTHORITY OVER SATAN

INTRODUCTION: God has promised to avenge us on human enemies, but we alone are responsible for dealing with Satan. We must command the devil to do what we demand, always using the name of Jesus.

Section One
PRAY THAT ALL CHRISTIANS WILL LEARN TO DEFEAT SATAN:

Complete these sentences:

1. Eph.1:17 (Pray that the Father) may give unto you the spirit of **WISDOM** and **REVELATION** in the knowledge of Him.

2. Eph.1:18 …(Pray to be enlightened to) know the hope of His **CALLING** and what the riches of the **GLORY** of His inheritance in the saints. (Every Christian has received authority over Satan if he knows how to appropriate it.)

3. Eph,1:19-21 …(Pray that fellow-believers will) know the exceeding greatness of His **POWER** to usward. (This is the same power which He wrought in Christ when He raised Him from the dead and set Him at His own **RIGHT HAND**, … far above all … (demonic) power and might and dominion, and every name that is named … in this **WORLD** and that … which is **TO COME**.

Section Two
DO YOUR JOB! TAKE AUTHORITY OVER SATAN!

When we were born again, God gave us authority in the spoken name of Jesus because:

4. Eph.2:10 We are His **WORKMANSHIP**, created in Christ Jesus unto **GOOD WORKS** (ie, God works) which God hath before ordained that we should walk in them.

5. Eph.3:10 (It was God's) intent that now unto the (demonic) **PRINCIPALITIES** and powers in heavenly places might be known by the **CHURCH** the manifold wisdom of God. (God asks us to demonstrate our authority over Sa-tan's entities so they will begin to tremble when a Christian opens his mouth.)

6. Eph.3:20 …He is able to do exceedingly abundantly above all that we **ASK** or think, (but He is limited by the) power that worketh in **US**. (If we do not use our mouth and the name of Jesus to appropriate the power He has provided, that power lies wasted.)

Section Three
TO MAINTAIN THE HIGHEST AUTHORITY OVER SATAN, WE SHOULD DO THE FOLLOWING:

7. Eph.4:1 …Walk worthy of the *VOCATION* with which ye were called. (ie, Recognize that Satan is your enemy. Do not go into his back yard unless called on by God to do so.)

8. Eph.4:2 (Walk) with all *LOWLINESS AND MEEKNESS,* with longsuffering, (bearing with) one another *IN LOVE.*

9. Eph.4:3-4 (Walk, always) endeavoring to keep the *UNITY* of the Spirit, just as you were called in *ONE HOPE* (and) one calling. ... (ie, Christians must remain in unity with their fellow-believers. We were called to this unity. If your church group is divisive and at unrest, find another church.)

10, Eph.4:13 …(because God wants His church to come into) the *UNITY OF THE FAITH,* and of the knowledge of the *SON OF GOD*, unto a perfect man, unto the measure of the stature of the *FULLNESS* of Christ.

11. Eph.5:6 Let no man deceive you with *VAIN WORDS*. (It is because of empty words that the) *WRATH* of God cometh on the children of *DISOBEDIENCE*.

12. Eph.5:19-21 (Keep your heart pure by) *SPEAKING* to yourselves in psalms, hymns, and spiritual songs, making melody in your *HEARTS* to the Lord, giving *THANKS* always for all things to God the Father in the *NAME* of our Lord Jesus Christ, *SUBMITTING* yourselves one to another in the fear of God.

Section Four
AND WE MUST . . .

13. Eph.6:10 Be strong in the Lord and in the power of *HIS MIGHT.*

14. Eph.6:13 Take unto you the whole *ARMOR OF GOD.*

15. I Pet.5:6 Humble yourself, therefore, under the mighty *HAND* of God that He may exalt you in *DUE TIME*.

16. I Pet.5:7 Casting all your care upon Him for He *CARETH* for you.

17. I Pet.5:8 Be sober, be vigilant, because your adversary the devil … walketh about **_SEEKING_** whom he may **_DEVOUR._**

LESSON FIVE
GOD'S HIGHER PLAN REQUIRES *AGAPE* LOVE

INTRODUCTION: The New Testament was written in the Greek language which has greater specificity in some of its words. For example, the Greek differentiates among the following words for "Love". (1) <u>*Agape* love</u> is the God-kind of love which flows from the Spirit of God within a Christian under the right conditions. (2) <u>Brotherly love</u> is love which flows from the soul.

Section One
JESUS COMMANDED CHRISTIANS TO HAVE *AGAPE* LOVE:

1. John 13:34 (Jesus said): A new **_COMMANDMENT_** I give unto you. That ye **_LOVE_** one another, as I have loved you, that ye also love one another. (*Agape Love*)

2. John 14:23 (Jesus made this promise): … If a man *agape* love Me, he will keep (obey) My **_WORDS_**; and My Father will **_LOVE_** him, and We will come unto him and make our abode **_WITH HIM_**. (Jesus commands that we *agape* love one another, and obey His voice. If a Christian does these two things, the Spirit of God and the Spirit of Christ will abide and work in him.)

Section Two
ONLY GOD CAN PRODUCE *AGAPE* LOVE:

3. Gal.5:22-23 (Christians cannot produce *agape* love independently of God because it is a fruit of the spirit. List the nine fruit): *Agape* **_LOVE, JOY, PEACE, LONGSUFFERING, GENTLENESS, GOODNESS, FAITH, MEEKNESS AND TEMPERANCE_**. (Notice that *agape* love is the first of the fruit which God sends into your heart, soul, and mind when conditions are right. He will not send the other eight until you have met the conditions for *agape* love.)

Section Three

TO RECEIVE *AGAPE* LOVE, I MUST PREPARE MY SOUL:

4. I Pet.1:22 (Peter teaches how to prepare one's soul. He said): Seeing ye have **PURIFIED** your souls in **OBEYING** the truth through the spirit unto unfeigned **LOVE** of the brethren, see that ye **LOVE** one another with a **PURE** heart fervently. (One way to purify your heart/soul/mind is to obey the Holy Spirit when He speaks to you. Another way is to brotherly love your fellowman; for when you do, God can use this seed to produce His fruit of *agape* love and the eight which follow.)

Section Four
WHY DOESN'T *AGAPE* LOVE FLOW EACH TIME I FEEL BROTHERLY LOVE?

5. Heb.13:1 (The Word answers the heading's question by saying): Let brotherly love **CONTINUE**. (If you do this, your seed of "continuing brotherly love" will germinate, just like any other seed.)

Section Five
HOW CAN YOU GENERATE BROTHERLY LOVE SEED?

6. Rom.12:14 (says to) **BLESS** them which **PERSECUTE** you; bless and **CURSE** not. (Regardless of how someone is treating you, you must speak blessings over him. In God's mysterious way, He causes your heart to soften when you audibly speak blessings. Then, He can begin to work on the one who hurt you, because you have loosed God to work His miracle in the other person also. Use discretion. Allow the person to hear you blessing him only if the Holy Spirit gives you permission to speak in his hearing. Usually this will be done in private, repeating it until you feel a breakthrough.)

7. Eph.5:20 (tells us to be): Giving **THANKS** always for **ALL** things unto God and the Father in the **NAME OF OUR LORD JESUS CHRIST**. (When bad things happen, audibly thank God for them. Yes, <u>thank</u> Him. He did not bring the bad thing on you, but when you thank and praise Him He is in a position to move heaven and earth to ease your situation. Use discretion. This is best done in private unless the person in your presence understands this practice and will not be offended. When you have continued in brotherly love for awhile, the Spirit of God will send agape love and the other eight spirit fruit into your heart/mind/soul.

Section Six

8. I John 2:10 He who *agape* loveth his brother abideth in the **LIGHT**, and there is none occasion of **STUMBLING** in him.

9. I John 3:14 We know that we have passed from **DEATH UNTO LIFE**, because we *agape* love the brethren. He that loveth not his brother abideth in **DEATH.**

LESSON SIX
GOD'S HIGHER PLAN REQUIRES REGULAR CHURCH ATTENDANCE

INTRODUCTION: Televised messages have their place for shut-ins; but God intended that His body, the church, meet together and minister to one another as the various parts of a human body take care of the other parts.

Section One
EVERY PART OF THE BODY NEEDS EVERY OTHER PART:

1. I Cor.12:12 As the (human) body is one and hath **MANY** members, and all the members of that one body, being many, are one body. So also is **CHRIST** (able to be in every Christian simultaneously.)

2. I Cor.12:13 For by one Spirit are we all baptized into one **BODY**, whether we be Jews or **GENTILES**, ... bond or free; and have been made to drink into one **SPIRIT.** (The Spirit of God baptizes all Christians into one body as part of the new birth. He provides the Spirit of Christ to give drinks of His anointing. Remember? Jesus told the woman at the well that He had water of which she knew not.)

3. I Cor.12:14-15 For the body is not one **MEMBER**, but many. If the foot shall say, "Because I am not the **HAND,** I am not part of the **BODY**; is it therefore not of the body.

4. I Cor.12:18 But now hath God set the members every one of them in the

body, as it hath **_PLEASED HIM_**. (We should be attending church where He sends us and serving as He leads.)

5. I Cor.12:26 Whether one member **_SUFFER_**, all the members suffer with it; or if one member be **_HONORED,_** all the members **_REJOICE_** with it. (Every church should be like this.)

6. I Cor. 12:27 Now ye are the **_BODY_** of Christ, and members in particular.

7. I Cor.12:28 List eight ministry functions which God assigns to each church body. **_APOSTLES, PROPHETS, TEACHERS, MIRACLES, GIFTS OF HEALINGS, HELPS, GOVERNMENTS, AND DIVERSITIES OF TONGUES._** (We should all be playing our part.)

Section Two
OTHER MINISTRY FUNCTIONS WE CAN QUALIFY FOR:

We can walk in love toward God:
8. I John 4:16 We have known and **_BELIEVED_** the love that God hath to us. God is **_LOVE,_** and he that dwelleth in love dwelleth in **_GOD_** and God in Him.

We can walk without fear:
9. I John 4:18 There is no **_FEAR_** in love; but **_PERFECT_** love casteth out fear; because … He that feareth is not made **_PERFECT IN LOVE_**.

We can walk in love toward fellow-Christians:
10. I John 4:20-21 If a man say "I **_LOVE GOD_**," and **_HATETH_** his brother, he is a **_LIAR_**. … And this commandment have we from Him, that he who loveth **_GOD_** love **_HIS BROTHER_** also.

We can walk as led by Christ, and not as dictated by church doctrine or the law:
11. Col.2:18 Let no man beguile (cheat) you of your **_REWARD_** in a voluntary (faked) and worshipping of **_ANGELS_**. … or (by being) vainly **_PUFFED UP_** by his fleshly mind.

12. Col.2:19-20 and not holding the **HEAD** (Christ), from which all the body ... increaseth with the of God. Wherefore if ye be **DEAD** with Christ from the rudiments of the world, why ... are you subject to ordinances (the law)?

13. Col.2:23 Which things have indeed a show of wisdom in (self- will worship), and (in) **HUMILITY**, and neglecting of the **BODY;** not in any honor to the satisfying of the **FLESH**. (These things appear to be spiritual, but they are not.)

<u>We can work in unity within the church body:</u>
14. Eph.4:13 (We must study the Word) till we all come in(to) the **UNITY** of the faith, and of the knowledge of the **SON OF GOD**, (growing) unto a **PERFECT** (mature) man, unto the measure of the stature of the fullness of **CHRIST.**

<u>We can be sure of what we believe and why we believe it:</u>
15. Eph.4:14 (We must study the Word and draw near to God so) that we henceforth be no more **CHILDREN** tossed to and fro, and carried about by every wind of **DOCTRINE**, by the sleight (trickery) of men ... whereby they lie in wait to **DECEIVE**.

<u>We can speak the truth in love to one another:</u>
16. Eph.4:15-16 (We must study the Word to know <u>the truth.</u> Then we must be) speaking the **TRUTH** in **LOVE** (so that we) may grow up into Him (Christ) in all things. ... from whom the whole body (is) fitly **JOINED TOGETHER** by that which every joint **SUPPLIETH**. ...

<u>We can share our time and our resources with fellow-believers who have needs:</u>
17. Acts 20:35 (We should follow Paul's example when he said): I have (shown) you all things ... how that ... ye ought to **SUPPORT** the weak and to remember the words of the Lord Jesus, how He said, ***"IT IS MORE BLESSED TO GIVE THAN TO RECEIVE."***

Section Three
BEGIN NOW TO DO THE FOLLOWING IN YOUR CHURCH:

<u>Encourage one another:</u>
18. Heb.3:13 Exhort one another *DAILY* ... lest any of you be hardened through the deceitfulness of *SIN.*

<u>And follow the example of the early church:</u>
19. Acts 2:42 (Continue steadfastly) in the apostles' *DOCTRINE* and *FELLOWSHIP,* and in *BREAKING OF BREAD,* and in *PRAYERS.*

LESSON SEVEN
GOD'S HIGHER PLAN REQUIRES PRAYER

INTRODUCTION: Pray when you are at home; pray when you go out. Pray when things look good; pray when things look bad. Paul says in I Thes.5:17 that we should pray without ceasing. Prayer takes many forms as evidenced below:

Section One
YOUR PRAYERS MUST INCLUDE PRAISE AND WORSHIP:
1. Heb.13:15 Let us offer the sacrifice of *PRAISE* to God continually, that is, the fruit of our *LIPS,* giving *THANKS* to His name.

2. Phil.3:3 For we are the (true) *CIRCUMCISION* which *WORSHIP* God in the Spirit, and *REJOICE* in Christ Jesus, and have no confidence in the *FLESH.*

3. Matt.6:9 (Jesus Himself told us to begin our prayers with worshipful praise): After this manner, therefore *PRAY* ye. Our Father which art in heaven, *HALLOWED* be thy name. ...

Section Two
YOU MUST TELL GOD WHAT YOU NEED AND THANK HIM IN ADVANCE:
4. Phil.4:6 Be careful (anxious) for nothing, but in everything by *PRAYER* and supplication with *THANKSGIVING,* let your requests be *MADE*

KNOWN unto God.

5. James 4:2-3 …(If ye do not have, it is because) ye ***ASK NOT,*** … (or) because ye ask amiss (with wrong motive) that ye may consume it upon your ***LUSTS***. (If you have prayed for some-thing and not received, it is because you asked for something you should not have.)

Section Three
YOU MUST INTERCEDE FOR THE NEEDS OF OTHERS, PRAY ALL KINDS OF PRAYER, AND WAIT PATIENTLY:

6. Eph.6:18 Praying always with all ***PRAYER AND SUPPLICATION*** in the Spirit, and watching thereunto with all ***PERSEVERANCE*** (patient continuance) and supplication for ***ALL SAINTS.***

7. Col.4:2 Continue in ***PRAYER,*** and watch in the same with ***THANKS-GIVING.***

8. I John 5:16 If any man see his brother sin a sin which is not unto ***DEATH,*** he shall ***ASK*** and (God) shall give him ***LIFE*** for them. … (However,) there is a sin not unto ***DEATH.*** I do not say he shall pray for it. (If a very mature Christian has knowingly and fully renounced Christ, the Holy Spirit will tell those who would pray for him that it is useless to do so.)

Section Four
YOU SHOULD OFFER UP THANKSGIVING FOR ALL THINGS:

9. Eph.5:20 (The Word instructs Christians to be) giving ***THANKS*** always for ***ALL THINGS*** unto God and the Father, in the name of our ***LORD JESUS CHRIST.***

10. I Thes.5:16-18 Rejoice ***EVERMORE!*** Pray ***WITHOUT CEASING.*** In everything ***GIVE THANKS,*** for this is the ***WILL OF GOD*** in Christ concerning you.

11. Rom.8:28 (This is the promise God has for those who are thankful in all circumstances): And we know that all things (will) work together for ***GOOD***

to them that *LOVE* God, to them who are *THE CALLED* according to His purpose. (This is God's promise: If you will thank Him in all circumstances, He will see that everything in life will work to your good.)

Section Five
YOU MUSTSPEAK IN FAITH:

12. Eph.6:16 Above all, taking the shield of *FAITH* wherewith ye shall be able to quench all the *FIERY DARTS* of the wicked (one).

13. I Pet.5:6-7 Humble yourselves therefore under the mighty *HAND* of God that He may *EXAULT* you in due time.

14. I Pet.5:8-9 (Be) *SOBER*, be *VIGILANT*; because your adversary the *DEVIL*, as a roaring *LION* walketh about, seeking whom he may *DEVOUR*. Whom resist, steadfast in the *FAITH* knowing that the same afflictions (problems) are accomplished in your brethren that are *IN THE WORLD*.

15. Matt.18:18 Jesus said: …Whatsoever ye shall *BIND* on earth shall be *BOUND* in heaven; and whatsoever ye shall *LOOSE* on earth shall be loosed in *HEAVEN*.

LESSON EIGHT
GOD'S HIGHER PLAN REQUIRES PATIENT SUFFERING

INTRODUCTION: Patience is a virtue highly esteemed by our Father. This is a study of patient suffering.

Section One
GOD IS OUR EXAMPLE OF PATIENCE, AS FOLLOWS:

1. Rom.2:4 (The Word says): Despiseth thou the riches of His *GOODNESS* and *FORBEARANCE* (patience) and *LONGSUFFERING*; not knowing

that the goodness of God leadeth thee to **REPENTANCE.** (God is our model of patience. He patiently waits for a person to turn to Him, thereby giving sufficient time for repentance.)

2. 2 Pet.3:15 Account that the longsuffering of our Lord is **SALVATION** – even as our beloved brother **PAUL** ... hath written unto you. (ie, Because of God's patience, many come to Christ and grow into maturity. When you are patient in the midst of sufferings, people will see Christ in you.)

3. Rom.9:22-23 What if God, willing to show His wrath (on the lost) and to make His known, endured with much longsuffering the vessels of wrath fitted to destruction (so) that He might make known the **POWER** of His glory on the vessels of mercy. ... (God does not take quick vengeance on the lost. Instead He allows the human race to continue in its ways so that those who are willing can come to Him.)

4. Rom.15:5 Now (may) the God of **PATIENCE** and **CONSOLATION** grant you to be likeminded one toward another, according to Christ Jesus. (We must be patient and nurturing with others just as God and Jesus are patient and nurturing with us.)

Section Two
GOD ASKS US TO PRACTICE PATIENCE ALSO:

5. Luke 8:15 (God says that "good grounds" are): they which (hear with) an **HONEST** and **GOOD** heart, (and) having heard the Word, keep it and bring forth fruit with **PATIENCE**. (A believer who has an honest and good heart will see his prayers answered if he continues to believe with patience.)

6. Luke 21:19 In your **PATIENCE** (you will be able to) **POSSESS** your souls. (ie, A person who can control his feelings while remaining patient is having control over his soul and thereby saving it.)

7. James 1:4 (The Word says that you must) let **PATIENCE** have her perfect work, that ye may be **PERFECT** and entire, wanting nothing. (ie, If a Christian can practice patience, he will be moving toward maturity.)

8. Eph.4:1-3 (The Word urges Christians to) *WALK* worthy of the vocation wherewith ye are *CALLED*, with all lowliness and meekness, with *LONG-SUFFERING*, forbearing one another in *LOVE*, endeavoring to keep the *UNITY* of the Spirit in the bond of *PEACE.*

9. 2 Thes.3:5 (You can remain patient and unified in love only with the help of God, so we pray: May) the Lord *DIRECT* your hearts into the love of God and into the patient *WAITING* for Christ.

10. I Tim.6:6 (Remember this): Godliness with *CONTENTMENT* is great *GAIN*. (Godliness and contentment can be sustained only by patient endurance.)

11. Heb.10:36 For ye have need of *PATIENCE* (so) that after ye have done the will of God, ye might receive the *PROMISE.* (It is God's will that you wait patiently while the promises are on their way to you.)

12. James 5:7 Be *PATIENT,* therefore, brethren, unto the *COMNG* of the Lord. …

13. James 5:8 Be ye also *PATIENT,* establish your *HEARTS,* for the coming of the Lord draweth nigh.

Section Three
FAITH MUST BE ADDED TO PATIENCE:

14. Heb.6:12 (The Word says): that ye be not slothful (sluggish and lazy), but be followers of them who through *FAITH* and patience inherit the *PROMISES.* (You should be familiar with the Bible heroes and follow their example.)

15. Tit.2:1-2 (You must): *SPEAK* thou the things which become sound doctrine. (We must encourage) the aged men (to) be sober, grave, temperate, sound in *FAITH*, in *CHARITY,* in *PATIENCE.*

16. Phil.4:6-7 (The Word says to): be *CAREFUL* (anxious) for nothing, but in everything, by *PRAYER* and supplication, with *THANKSGIVING,* let

your requests be made known unto God; and the ***PEACE*** of God which passeth all under-standing, shall keep your ***HEARTS*** and ***MINDS*** through Christ Jesus. (Speak rebuke to fear and anxiety – in the name of Jesus.)

17. 2 Pet.1:5-7 And beside this, giving all ***DILIGENCE***, add to your faith ***VIRTUE***; and (add) to your virtue ***KNOWLEDGE;*** and (add) to your knowledge ***TEMPERANCE*** (self-control); and (add) to your temperance ***PATIENCE***; and (add) to your patience ***GODLINESS;*** and (add) to godliness brotherly kindness; and (add) to brotherly kindness ***CHARITY*** (ie, *agape love)*. (All of these attributes issue from a pure heart. Purity of heart is essential to successful Christian maturity.)

Section Four
FAITH PLUS PATIENCE EQUALS "HOPE":

18. Rom.8:25 (God says): If we ***HOPE*** for that we see not, then do we with ***PATIENCE*** wait for it.

Section Five
KNOW THAT GODLY PEOPLE WILL SUFFER AT TIMES:

19. 2 Tim.3:12 (Paul told Timothy): … all that will live ***GODLY*** in Christ Jesus shall suffer ***PERSECUTION.***

20. 2 Thes.1:4 (Paul told the churches of God: We glory in you for your) ***PATIENCE*** and ***FAITH*** in all your ***PERSECUTIONS*** and tribulations that ye endure.

Section Six
YOU MUST REJOICE DURING SUFFERINGS:

21. James 1:2-3 My brethren, ***COUNT IT ALL JOY*** when ye fall into diverse ***TEMPTATIONS,*** knowing this, that the trying of your ***FAITH*** worketh ***PATIENCE.*** (When you fall into trials, audibly rejoice! God will reward this.)

22. I Pet.1:6-7 Wherein ye greatly ***REJOICE*** though now for a season, if need be, ye are in heaviness through manifold ***TEMPTATIONS*** that the trial of your ***FAITH*** … might be found unto ***PRAISE*** and ***HONOR*** and glory

at the appearing of Jesus Christ (at the rapture).

23. Eph.5:20 Giving **THANKS** always for **ALL THINGS** unto God and the Father in the **NAME** of our Lord Jesus Christ. (Audibly thank God, regardless of how things look around you.)

24. Rom.12:14 (And) **BLESS** them which **PERSECUTE** you; bless and curse not.

LESSON NINE
GOD'S HIGHER PLAN REQUIRES TWO KINDS OF RIGHTEOUSNESS

INTRODUCTION: Why does God require shed blood and belief in Jesus Christ for all, yet He has a Higher Plan which all Christians should press toward? The answer to that question is that God has two kinds of righteousness. The first kind of righteousness is the "Righteousness of God". The second kind of righteousness is the "Righteousness of Christ" This is a study of the two, their meanings, and their rewards.

Section One
THE "RIGHTEOUSNESS OF GOD" IS THE "NEW BIRTH":

The new birth is available only through belief in the shed blood of Christ:

1. John 3:3 (Jesus said): … I say unto thee, except a man be **BORN AGAIN**, he cannot see the **KINGDOM OF GOD**.

2. John 3:5 (Jesus added): … Except a man be born of the **WATER** and of the **SPIRIT**, he cannot enter into the kingdom of God. (There are two ways of understanding this verse: Born of water can mean being physically birthed from your mother; or it can mean being born again by hearing, believing, and confessing the gospel of Christ. The Word is referred to as washing water throughout the New Testament. To be born the second time is to accept Jesus Christ as your Savior. Unless the new birth occurs, you will not/cannot go to heaven and live eternally with God and Jesus Christ.)

Section Two
HOW IS THE NEW BIRTH ACCOMPLISHED?

3. Rom.10:9-10 …If thou shalt ***CONFESS*** with thy mouth the Lord Jesus and shalt ***BELIEVE*** in thine heart that God hath ***RAISED HIM*** from the dead, thou shalt be saved. For with the ***HEART*** man believeth unto righteousness; and with the ***MOUTH*** confession is made unto salvation. (A person is born again and receives the righteousness of God by having faith in Jesus Christ and confessing his belief audibly.)

Section Three
OTHER SCRIPTURE WHICH SPEAK OF THE NEW BIRTH RIGHTEOUSNESS OF GOD:

4. Rom.3:20-22 Therefore, by the deeds of the ***LAW*** there shall no flesh be justified in His sight. For by the law is (merely) the ***KNOWLEDGE*** of sin. But now the righteousness of God without the law is manifested, being witnessed by the law and the prophets. Even the righteousness of God which is by ***FAITH*** of Jesus Christ. …

5. Rom.1:16-17 (Paul said): … I am not ashamed of the gospel of Christ, for it is the ***POWER*** of God unto salvation to everyone that ***BELIEVETH***. … (For in the gospel of Christ) is the righteousness of God revealed from ***FAITH TO FAITH***. … The just shall ***LIVE*** by faith.

6. Rom.10:3 (Israel refused the new birth righteousness of God when they crucified the Messiah.) For they being ignorant of God's righteousness, and going about to ***ESTABLISH*** their own righteousness, have not ***SUBMITTED*** themselves to the righteousness of God. (If you have been born again, you are a true Christian. If you have not taken this critical step, take a moment and appropriate Romans 10:9-10 above. You must audibly confess your acceptance of Jesus Christ as the risen Son of God. Just as God spoke the worlds into place. We speak our new world into place.)

Section Four
THE NEW BIRTH OCCURS IN MAN'S SPIRIT:

Man is spirit, soul, and body: The new birth occurs in the innermost part of man, called the spirit. When you confess Jesus Christ as described above, the Spirit of God comes and dwells in your new spirit. The born-again spirit cannot sin.

7. I Cor. 3:16 Know ye not that ye are the **TEMPLE OF GOD**, and that the **SPIRIT OF GOD** dwelleth in you? (Old Testament believers were incapable of having the righteousness of God because the Spirit of God could not dwell in mankind before Jesus paid the price with His blood.)

Section Five
THE "RIGHTEOUSNESS OF CHRIST" IS THE RENEWING OF THE SOUL:

The soul is the second part of mankind: The soul consists of a person's heart and mind. When the Word speaks of heart, mind, or soul, it is referring to the soul of man.

8. 3 John 2 (God wants the soul of every Christian to prosper. John, the apostle, wrote): Beloved, I wish **ABOVE ALL THINGS** that thou mayest prosper and be in health, even as thy **SOUL** prospereth. (Any physician can tell you that a heart and mind at peace is much more likely to have a healthy body and a productive life.)

Section Six
VERSES ABOUT THE "RIGHTEOUSNESS OF CHRIST":

Match each verse to its proper address:

__C__ 9. I die to the law that I might live to God's voice .   A. Col.2:6-7

__E__ 10. You have a choice: Either yield your body to righteousness or to iniquity.   B. Gal.2:20

__F__ 11. Righteousness by faith is a day-by-day goal.   C. Gal.2:19

__A__ 12. The righteousness of Christ is attained through walking by faith in Jesus Christ.   D. Gal.3:5

__D__ 13. God is able to minister to you and work

miracles through your faith, not the law. E. Rom.6:19

__B__ 14. When I crucify myself, Christ lives
in and through me. F. Gal.5:5

Section Seven
OLD TESTAMENT RIGHTEOUSNESS OF CHRIST:
The Righteousness of Christ was available in the Old Testament because man has always had a soul:

15. Gen.2:7 The Lord God ***FORMED*** man of the dust of the ground, and ***BREATHED*** into his nostrils the breath of life, and man became a living soul (or living being).

16. Heb.11:7 (Noah is one of many Old Testament saints who were accounted as having the righteousness of Christ.) By ***FAITH*** Noah … prepared an ark to the saving of his house, by the which he condemned the world, and became ***HEIR*** of the righteousness which is by ***FAITH.***

LESSON TEN
GOD'S HIGHER PLAN REQUIRES CHRISTIANS WHO SHINE FOR HIM

INTRODUCTION: If you are a Christian, you are a lighthouse. Is your light shining bright? Can others find their way by keeping their eyes on you? The purpose of this lesson is to teach every Christian to become high voltage, bright lighthouses for those around them.

Section One
TO BECOME A SHINING LIGHTHOUSE, DO THE FOLLOWING:
Determine you want to be the light of Christ and not self. Seek His leading and you will shine like a beacon.

1. John 8:12 (Jesus said): I am the ***LIGHT*** of the world. He who followeth

Me (follows my quiet leadings) shall not walk in *DARKNESS,* but shall have the *LIGHT OF LIFE*. (Determine to use Jesus as your role model. He repeatedly said that He did nothing but what the Father told him to do.)

Eliminate complaining and disputing from your life, and hold fast to the truth that is in Jesus Christ and His Word.
2. Phil.2:14-16 (The Word teaches): Do all things without *MURMERINGS AND DISPUTINGS* that ye may be blameless and harmless, the *SONS OF GOD* without rebuke in the midst of a crooked and perverse nation among whom ye *SHINE* as lights in the *WORLD*. ("Murmering" is complaining)

Monitor your thoughts and your behavior.
3. I Thes.5:4-6 But ye, brethren, are not in *DARKNESS*, that that day should overtake you as a *THIEF*. Ye are all the children of *LIGHT*; we are not of the *NIGHT* or darkness. Therefore, let us not sleep … but let us watch and be *SOBER.*

Practice "Faith plus Hope equals *Agape* Love" to appropriate Holy Spirit oil.
4. I Thes.5:8-9 Let us who are of the *DAY* be sober, putting on the breastplate of *FAITH AND LOVE*, and for an helmet the *HOPE* of salvation by our Lord Jesus Christ. (A breastplate covers both the spirit and soul of a Christian. Thus, the words used to fill in these blanks list the elements of a breastplate of righteousness.)

Keep your armor in place.
5. Eph.6:13 …Take unto you the whole armor of God, that you may be able to *WITHSTAND* in the evil day, and having done *ALL* (the Word tells you to do), to stand.

6. Eph.6:14 Stand therefore, having your loins girt about with *TRUTH*, and having on the *BREASTPLATE OF RIGHTEOUSNESS*. (The truth is God's Word – what He speaks to you and what He has written in Scripture. You "stand" when you know and practice "the truth" and your spirit and soul are covered with the breastplate of righteousness.)

7. Eph.6:15 (Shod your feet) with the preparation of the gospel of **PEACE**. (God's truth is a message of peace. You must know God's words about peace and walk accordingly.)

8. Eph.6:16 Above all, taking the shield of **FAITH** wherewith ye shall be able to quench all the **FIERY DARTS** of the wicked (one). (Satan puts wicked thoughts into your mind, and he uses his people to send tribulation into your life.)

9. Eph.6:17 And take the helmet of **SALVATION** (a renewed mind.) and the sword of the Spirit which is the **WORD OF GOD**. (When a believer speaks the Word of God with authority, using the name of Jesus, the spoken word acts as a sword to cut away Satan's attacks.)

10. Eph.6:18 Praying always with all (kinds of) **PRAYER** and supplication in the Spirit, and **WATCHING** thereunto with all perseverance and supplication for all saints. (Pray in the Spirit, and pray for your fellow-believers.)

Section Two
WHAT MUST WE DO TO KEEP OUR LAMPS FULL?

Continually give praises to God, knowing that the oil comes from the Holy Spirit and not from yourself.

11. Col.1:12 (Your lamp shines when you thank Him): Giving **THANKS** unto the Father, which has made us meet to be partakers of the inheritance of the saints in **LIGHT**. (When you speak thanksgivings to God, your light turns on and you become a recipient of the promises due to those who walk in the light.)

Share your blessings with others while deflecting all glory onto the Father and the Son – never keep it for yourself.

12. Matt.5:14 (Jesus said): Ye are the **LIGHT** of the world. A city that is set on a hill cannot be **HID**. (A person whose light is shining is as apparent to others as a city sitting on a hill.)

13. Matt.5:16 Let your light so **SHINE** before men, that they may see your

good works and *GLORIFY* your Father which is in heaven. ("Good works" are works which a Christian does in obedience to God's voice. When others notice, you must be sure that you deflect all glory to God, and not self.)

Stay in the word daily. The word creates oil for your lamp/lighthouse.
14. Luke 12:35 (Jesus said): Let your loins be girded about (with the truth), and your *LIGHTS BURNING*.

15. Luke 11:35 (Jesus also said): Take heed therefore that the *LIGHT* which is in thee is not *DARKNESS*. (Do not attempt to fake light; otherwise you produce darkness. The Spirit within you is the source of true light.)

LESSON ELEVEN
GOD'S HIGHER PLAN REQUIRES HUMILITY

INTRODUCTION: Individuals, as well as nations, must humble themselves before God.

Section One
WHAT MUST A NATION DO?

1. 2 Chron.7:14 (God says): If My people which are called by My name shall *HUMBLE* themselves and *PRAY* and *SEEK* My face and *TURN* from their wicked ways, then will I *HEAR* from heaven, and will forgive their sin and will *HEAL* their land.

Section Two
GOD SAYS WE MUST HUMBLE OURSELVES:•

<u>Because pride deceives the heart:</u>
2. Oba.1:3 (God says): The pride of thine heart hath *DECEIVED* thee, thou that dwelleth in the clefts of the rock, whose habitation is *HIGH*, that saith in his heart, Who shall bring me *DOWN* to the ground.

<u>Because pride in the heart defiles the whole man:</u>
3. Mark 7:20-23 (Jesus says): That which cometh *OUT OF* the man, that

DEFILETH the man. For from within, out of the heart of men, proceed ***EVIL THOUGHTS,*** etc. ... All these evil things come from ***WITHIN*** and defile the man.

Because pride of heart is worldly:
4. I John 2:16 For all that is in the world -- the lust of the ***FLESH***, and the lust of the ***EYES***, and the ***PRIDE*** of life is not of the Father, but is of the ***WORLD***.

And: Because pride brings destruction and failure:
5. Prov.16:18 Pride goeth before ***DESTRUCTION,*** and a haughty spirit before a ***FALL.***

6. Prov.16:19 Better it is to be of a ***HUMBLE*** spirit with the lowly than to divide the spoil with the ***PROUD.***

The humble are more likely to be rich in faith:
7. James 2:5 ...Hath not God chosen the ***POOR*** of this world (to be) rich in ***FAITH*** and heirs of the kingdom which hath He promised to them that ***LOVE*** Him. (God chose the poor to be the primary recipient of His grace.)

8. James. :6 God resisteth the ***PROUD*** but giveth grace to the ***HUMBLE***.

9. James 4:10 (So) ***HUMBLE*** yourselves in the sight of the Lord, and He shall ***LIFT YOU UP.***

The humble are in a position to be exalted:
10. I Pet.5:6 (God says): Humble yourselves therefore under the mighty hand of God, that ***HE*** may exalt you in due time.

The humble increase their joy:
11. Isa.29:19 The meek also shall ***INCREASE*** their joy in the Lord, and the ***POOR*** among men shall rejoice in the Holy One of Israel.

The humble Christian will walk as follows:

12. Eph.4:1-3 … Walk worthy of the vocation wherewith ye are called, with all ***LOWLINESS***, with longsuffering, ***FORBEARING*** one another in love, endeavoring to keep the unity of the Spirit in the ***BOND*** of peace.

13. Rom.12:2 And be not conformed to this ***WORLD***, but be ye ***TRANSFORMED*** by the ***RENEWING*** of your mind, that you may prove what is that good and acceptable and perfect ***WILL OF GOD***.

Section Three
GOD PLEADS WITH YOU TO COME TO HIM IN HUMILITY:
Sincere prayer is evidence of humility:
14. Matt.26:41 (Jesus said): ***WATCH*** and ***PRAY***, that ye enter not into temptation. (When you pray, you demonstrate your dependence on God.)

Confession of sins is evidence of humility:
15. I John 1:9 For if we ***CONFESS*** our sins, He is faithful and just to ***FORGIVE*** us our sins and to ***CLEANSE*** us from all unrighteousness.

LESSON TWELVE
GOD'S HIGHER PLAN REQUIRES FORGIVING AND BEING FORGIVEN

INTRODUCTION: A pure heart is a heart which rests in peace and goodwill toward God and others. God desires that every Christian walk in peace.

Section One
SCRIPTURE REQUIRING GOODWILL TOWARD OTHERS:
1. Col.3:12 Put on therefore, as the elect of God, holy and beloved, bowels of ***MERCIES***, (and) ***KINDNESS***, humbleness of mind, meekness, (and) long-suffering.

Section Two
SCRIPTURE REQUIRING FORGIVENESS TOWARD OTHERS:

2. Col.3:13   Forbearing one another and   ***FORGIVING ONE ANOTHER***; if any man have a quarrel against any; even as   ***CHRIST FORGAVE***   you, so also do ye.

Section Three
SCRIPTURE REQUIRING GOODNESS TOWARD OTHERS:

3. Col.3:14   And above all these things put on   ***CHARITY,***   which is the bond of perfection.

Section Four
SCRIPTURE REQUIRING A HEART OF PEACE:

4. Col.3:15   And let the   ***PEACE OF GOD***   rule in your hearts, to the which also ye   ***ARE CALLED***   in one body; and be ye   ***THANKFUL***.

Section Five
WHAT DID JESUS TEACH ABOUT FORGIVENESS?

5. Matt.18:21   (Peter came to Jesus and said): "Lord, how oft shall my brother sin against me, and I   ***FORGIVE HIM?***   Till   ***SEVEN***   times?"

6. Matt.18:22   (Jesus answered): "I say not unto thee, "Until seven times; but (I say) "Until   ***SEVENTY TIMES SEVEN.***   (I must forgive without end, both for the offender's sake and mine.)

7. Mark 11:25-26   (Jesus said): And when ye stand praying,   ***FORGIVE,***   if ye have aught against any;   ***THAT YOUR FATHER***   also which is in heaven ***MAY FORGIVE***   you your trespasses. But if ye do not   ***FORGIVE***, neither will your Father which is in heaven ***FORGIVE YOUR TRESPASSES.***

Section Six
WHAT DID JESUS TEACH ABOUT CLEARING A DISAGREEMENT WITH A FELLOW CHRISTIAN?

8. Luke 17:3-4   (When you are sure you have forgiven your brother, but he continues to be offending, you may do the following): Take heed to yourselves. (Get your heart right!) If thy brother trespass against thee,   ***REBUKE HIM;***   and if he repent,   ***FORGIVE HIM.***   ... (Tell him what he is repeatedly doing that is hurtful to you.) If he repents, (tell him you) forgive him.

9. Luke 17:5 (The apostles felt this was humanly impossible, so they said to the Lord): ***INCREASE OUR FAITH.*** (If forgiveness seems too difficult for you as well, pray these words from the apostles.)

10. Luke 17:6 (So, Jesus taught the apostles how to increase their faith and see their unforgiveness disappear.) If ye had ***FAITH*** as a grain of mustard seed, ye might ***SAY*** unto the sycamine tree, (representing unforgiveness), "Be thou ***PLUCKED UP*** by the root, and be thou ***CAST*** in the sea, and it should obey you. (Say, " In the precious name of Jesus Christ, I command Satan and his unforgiveness to leave my body and be cast into the sea.")

11. Matt.5.44 (Jesus said):… Love your ***ENEMIES.*** Bless them that ***CURSE*** you. Do ***GOOD*** to them that hate you, and ***PRAY*** for them which despitefully use you and persecute you.

Section Seven
WHAT ELSE DID JESUS TEACH ABOUT DISPUTES?

12. Matt.18:15 (Jesus said): … If thy brother shall ***TRESPASS*** against thee, (ie, takes your property or harms it), go and ***TELL HIM*** his fault between thee and him alone. If he shall hear thee (and replaces your property), thou hast gained thy brother.

13. Matt.18:16 But if he will not ***HEAR THEE*** thee, then take with thee one or two more (who are witnesses to the crime) that in the ***MOUTH*** of two or three witnesses, ***EVERY WORD*** (you say) may be ***ESTABLISHED.***

14. Matt.18:17 And if he shall ***NEGLECT*** to hear them, tell it unto the church (leadership). But if he neglect to hear the ***CHURCH,*** let him be unto thee as an ***HEATHERN*** man and a publican. (The Old Testament Jews were allowed to take foreigners and tax collectors before governmental judges. The Christian is permitted to take the offender to court at this point.)

15. I Cor.6:7 (Paul taught that it is a no-win situation for all if a Christian takes a brother before a heathen court. He said):… Why do you not rather suffer yourselves to be ***DEFRAUDED***?

Section Eight
TO ACCOMPLISH TRUE FORGIVENESS WITHIN
THE HEART – SPEAK BLESSINGS ON THE OFFENDER:

16. Matt.5:44 (Jesus said): … ***BLESS*** them that curse you, ***DO GOOD*** to them that hate you, and ***PRAY FOR*** them that spitefully use you.

Section Nine
TO ENSURE THAT GOD CONTINUES TO FORGIVE
YOUR SINS – CONFESS EACH SIN TO HIM

17. I John 1:9 If we ***CONFESS*** our sins, he is faithful and just to ***FORGIVE US*** our sins, and , and to ***CLEANSE US*** from all unrighteousness.

LESSON THIRTEEN
GOD'S HIGHER PLAN REQUIRES TITHING

INTRODUCTION: Are you financially strapped? God's Word has the answer to every solution. He desires to see His children prosper, and his Word tell us how.

Section One
IF YOU DESIRE TO PROSPER FINANCIALLY YOU
MUST PLANT YOUR TITHE SEED EVERY WEEK:

1. Mal.3:10 (God's Word says): Bring ye all the ***TITHES*** into the storehouse that there may be meat in Mine ***HOUSE,*** Prove Me now herewith, saith the Lord, … if I will not open you the windows of ***HEAVEN*** and pour you out a blessing, that there shall not be room enough to receive it.

2. Mal.3:11 (When you give to God, He promises to): ***REBUKE THE DEVOURER*** (Satan) for your sakes, so that he will not destroy the ***FRUITS*** of your ground.

Section Two
IF YOU ARE NOT TITHING, PRAY FOR STRENGTH TO START:

3. I Cor.2:5 (Pray) that your ***FAITH*** should not stand in the wisdom of men, but in the ***POWER OF GOD.***

4. James 1:5-6 (Pray for wisdom to know what to pray, because): If any of you lack wisdom, let him *ASK OF GOD* that giveth to all men liberally and upbraideth not; and it shall be given him. … But let him *ASK IN FAITH* … .

5. I Cor.1:25 (Recognize the need for God's help, because): the foolishness of God is *WISER* than men; and the weakness of God is *STRONGER* than men.

6. I Cor.1:30 Of Him are ye in Christ Jesus, who… is made unto us *WISDOM* and righteousness and sanctification and redemption.

7. I Cor.3:19 For the wisdom of this *WORLD* is *FOOLISHNESS* with God.. ..

Section Three
YOU MUST CURB YOUR WASTEFUL SPENDING BY:

8. Col.3:16 (Letting) the *PEACE OF GOD* dwell in you richly in all wisdom. ... (ie, Stay in the Word.)

Section Four
CURB YOUR SPENDING BY THANKING GOD FOR THE THINGS YOU HAVE NOW:

9. Psa.100:2 (The Word says to): Serve the Lord with *GLADNESS;* come before His presence with *SINGING.*

10. Col.3:15 And let the peace of God rule in your *HEARTS,* to the which …ye are *CALLED,* … and be thankful.

11. Eph.5:20 Giving thanks always for *ALL* things unto God …in the *NAME* of our Lord Jesus Christ.

12. Phil.4:6 (We are told to never worry), but in every thing, by *PRAYER* and supplication, with *THANKSGIVING,* let your requests be made known unto God.

13. Heb.13:15 By Him therefore, let us offer the sacrifice of *PRAISE* to God *CONTINUALLY,* ... giving thanks to His name.

14. 2 Cor.2:14   Now thanks be unto God which always causeth us to **TRIUMPH**   in Christ ...

15. I Cor.15:57 But   **THANKS**   be to God which giveth us the   **VICTORY**   through our Lord Jesus Christ.

Section Five
COMMIT TO PRACTICING SELF-CONTROL THAT:

16. 2 Pet.1:4-8   ...ye might be partakers of the   **DIVINE NATURE,**   having escaped the corruption that is in the world through   **LUST.**

17. I Pet.2:11   ...Fleshly lusts war against the   **SOUL.**

Section Six
COMMIT TO SHARE WITH THOSE IN NEED:

18. Eph.4:28 (Do not steal. Work with your hands that you) may have   **TO GIVE**   to him that   **NEEDETH.**

Section Seven
I COMMIT TO THE FOLLOWING PRIORITIES:

19. I will give God the first ten percent every week.

20. I will put ten percent in savings every week, and live on the remaining eighty percent.

21. My gifts to others will come out of my living allowance or savings account.

LESSON FOURTEEN
GOD'S HIGHER PLAN REQUIRES
TWO OCCUPIED ROOMS -- I

INTRODUCTION: If you are a Christian, you are the living, breathing temple of God. You are His three-part tabernacle on earth. You are spirit, soul, and body. Heaven's plan is: That the Spirit of God occupy your spirit room; that the Spirit of Christ occupy your soul room; and that you occupy and master your flesh with God's help.

Section One
THIS IS HOW THE OLD TESTAMENT TABERNACLE LOOKED:
(The outer court is not pictured in Sections One and Two.)

HOLY PLACE	MOST HOLY PLACE

Section Two
THIS IS HOW (YOU) THE NEW TESTAMENT TABERNACLE LOOKS TO GOD:

HEART MIND (SOUL)	BORN AGAIN (SPIRIT)

Section Three
INFORMATION ABOUT THE CHRISTIAN'S SPIRIT:

Your new spirit was prophesied by Jeremiah and described in Hebrews:

1. Heb.8:10 …(God promised to put His laws in their) ***MINDS*** and write them in their ***HEARTS***; and I will be to them a God and they shall be to Me a ***PEOPLE.***

God's Spirit cannot dwell in a person until God prepares a new place for His Spirit:

Jesus taught about the change which comes about as soon as a person asks Jesus Christ to be his personal Lord and Savior.

2. Mark 2:22 … No man putteth new ***WINE*** into old bottles; else the new wine doth burst the bottles, and the wine is spilled, and the bottles will be marred; but ***NEW WINE*** must be put into ***NEW BOTTLES***. (Your new spirit place is the new bottle. God's Spirit within your new spirit is the new wine)

When the new place has been prepared, the Spirit of God comes in and the new **birth occurs. All this can happen in a moment's time:**

3. I Cor.3:16   Know ye not that ye are the   ***TEMPLE OF GOD***.   and that the Spirit of God dwelleth in   ***YOU?***

The Spirit of God will speak to you from within your new spirit. Your job is to listen and obey:
4. Rom.8:14   For as many as are   ***LED***   by the Spirit of God, they are sons of ***GOD.***

The moment you are born again, you are pure throughout your spirit and soul, regardless of your past:
5. I Cor.6:11   Paul said: (You were many evil things before), but ye are washed, but ye are sanctified (set apart for God's use), but ye are justified in the   ***NAME***   of the Lord Jesus Christ, and by the   ***SPIRIT***   of our God.

As a born-again Christian, you have access to the following promise:
6. I Cor.6:12   …All things are   ***LAWFUL***   for me, but I will not be brought under the   ***POWER OF ANY.***

Section Four
INFORMATION ABOUT THE CHRISTIAN'S SOUL:
Three words refer to all, or part, of the soul of man:
You are responsible for keeping your <u>heart/mind/soul</u> clean so that God can use you:

THE MIND:
7. Rom.12:2   Be not conformed to this   ***WORLD***,   but be ye transformed by the renewing of your   ***MIND***,   that ye may prove what is that good and accept-able and perfect   ***WILL***   of God.

8. I Pet.1:13   Wherefore gird up the loins of your mind. Be sober, and hope to the end for the   ***GRACE***   that is to be brought to you at the (revealing) of ***JESUS CHRIST.***

9. Eph.4:22-23   …Put off concerning the former conversation the   ***OLD MAN*** which is   ***CORRUPT***   according to the deceitful lusts, and be   ***RENEWED*** in the spirit of your mind.

THE HEART:

10. Heb 10:22 Let us draw near (to God) with a *** TRUE HEART *** in full assurance of faith, having our *** HEARTS *** sprinkled from an evil conscience and our bodies washed with pure water. (ie, the Word)

11. 2 Cor.1:21-22 He which establisheth us with you in Christ and has anointed us is *** GOD, *** who hath also sealed us and given (us) the earnest of *** THE SPIRIT *** (of Christ) in our hearts. (When a Christian keeps the Spirit of Christ flowing in his heart most of the time, he is guaranteed not to fall away.)

THE SOUL:

12. Heb.10:39 But we are not of them who draw back unto *** PERDITION, *** but of them that believe to the saving of the *** SOUL. *** (Saving of the soul is an ongoing process of renewing the mind and purifying the heart.)

13. 3 John 2 Beloved, I wish above all things that thou mayest *** PROSPER *** and be in health, even as thy *** SOUL *** prospereth.

<u>A CHRISTIAN'S SPIRIT ROOM:</u> The Spirit of God dwells in a Christian's new spirit from the moment he was born again.

Section Five
THE CHRISTIAN'S SOUL ROOM:

God will send the Spirit of Christ into your soul room as often as you prepare it for His entry.

14. Rev.3:20 Jesus said: Behold, I stand at the door and *** KNOCK. *** If any man hear My voice and open the *** DOOR, *** I will come *** IN *** to him and sup with him and he with Me. (Jesus spoke these words to the church – born-again Christians. The Spirit of Christ wants to spend more time in your heart/mind/soul room.)

There is a doorway between your spirit room and your soul room:

15. John 10:2 He (the Spirit of Christ) that entereth in by the *** DOOR *** is the *** SHEPHERD *** of the flock.

16. John 10:3 To Him the porter openeth and the sheep (you and I) hear His ***VOICE;***   and He calleth His own sheep by name and   ***LEADETH THEM*** out.   (The Spirit of Christ desires to speak to you and lead you in all your ways.)

Section Six
THE DOORWAY BETWEEN THE CHRISTIAN'S SPIRIT AND SOUL:
God desires to see your doorway open at all times:

17. Eph.3:14 For this cause I ***BOW*** my knees unto the ***FATHER*** of our Lord Jesus Christ.

18. Eph.3:16 That He would grant you, according to the riches of His glory, to be ***STRENGTHENED*** with might by His (Christ's) Spirit in the ***INNER MAN***.

19. Eph.3:17 That ***CHRIST*** (the Spirit of Christ) may dwell in your hearts by ***FAITH;***   that ye, being rooted and grounded in love...

20. Eph.3:18-19 … may be able to comprehend with all saints what is the … love of Christ which passeth ***KNOWLEDGE,*** that ye might be filled with all the ***FULLNESS*** of God. (You are filled with the fullness of God when you have the Spirit of God in your born-again spirit, the Spirit of Christ in your heart/mind/soul, and the Holy Spirit in and around you.)

21. 2 Cor.5:17 Therefore, if any man be in Christ, he is a ***NEW CREATURE***. …

Section Seven
WHY SHOULD I KEEP THE SPIRIT OF CHRIST IN MY SOUL ROOM AS OFTEN AS POSSIBLE?

22. John 15:4 Jesus said: Abide in ***ME***   and I in you (your soul room). As the (tree) branch cannot ***BEAR FRUIT*** of itself except it abide in the vine, no more can ye, except ye ***ABIDE IN ME.*** (ie, abide in the Spirit of Christ.)

23. John 15:6 If a man abide not in ***ME,***   he is cast out as a branch and is ***WITHERED***. … (When your heart has become soiled, the Spirit of Christ must vacate the soul room. When that happens, your soul becomes estranged and it

begins to wither.)

Section Eight
THE OLD TABERNACLE VERSUS THE NEW:

No one except the high priest could approach God in the Old Testament tabernacle, and that happened only once a year. The Spirit of God lives in every born-again Christian. We can approach God at any time – night or day. He is always there. Our job is to commune with Him. When we do, we cleanse the soul room so that the Spirit of Christ can flow in, and then out to others, like "rivers of living water".

LESSON FIFTEEN
GOD'S HIGHER PLAN REQUIRES
TWO OCCUPIED ROOMS -- II

INTRODUCTION: If you are a Christian, you are the living, breathing temple of God today. The Spirit of God dwells in every born-again Christian. The Spirit of Christ will dwell in every Christian's soul if he sanctifies the area by speaking sincere words to God. As soon as a person is born again, he is righteous in his spirit room. His goal should be to be righteous in his soul room as regularly as possible.

Section One
PAUL CALLED THIS PROCESS "THE FELLOWSHIP MYSTERY":

1. Eph.3:8-9 (Paul said): ... (To me is this grace given) that I should ***PREACH*** among the Gentiles the unsearchable riches of Christ, and to make all men see what is the ***FELLOWSHIP*** of the mystery which from the beginning of the world hath been hid in God ... . (Here, Paul referred to the two rooms and their purpose within the Christian.)

2. Eph.6:12 For we wrestle not against ***FLESH*** and blood, but against principalities and powers, and against the ***RULERS OF THE DARKNESS*** of this world ... . (The Spirit of God and the Spirit of Christ are in a Christian for the purpose of helping him overcome Satan and his demons on a moment-by-moment basis.)

Section Two

THE SPIRIT OF CHRIST WILL SPEAK TO YOU
WHEN YOU ACCEPT SATAN'S TEMPTATIONS:

3. Heb.12:6 Whom the Lord loves, He *CHASTENETH* ... . (God speaks to the Christian's conscience.)

4. Heb.12:11 Now no *CHASTENING* for the present seemeth to be joyous ... nevertheless, afterward it yieldeth the peaceable *FRUIT OF RIGHTEOUSNESS* unto them which are exercised thereby.

Section Three
HIS CHASTENING IS TO REMIND US TO ALWAYS:

5. Heb.12:14 Follow *PEACE* with all men, and *HOLINESS*, without which no man shall see the Lord (work).

Section Four
WHEN HE POINTS OUT A SIN, DO THE FOLLOWING:

6. I John 1:9 If we confess our *SINS*, He is *FAITHFUL* and just to forgive us our sins and to *CLEANSE* us from all unrighteousness.

7. Eph.5:20 Giving *THANKS* always for all things unto God and the Father in the *NAME* of our Lord Jesus Christ.

8. Rom.12:14 *BLESS* them which persecute you; bless and curse not.

9. I Cor.4:12-13 ... Being reviled, we *BLESS*; being persecuted, we suffer it (patiently). Being defamed, we *ENTREAT* ...

Section Five
THE SPIRIT OF CHRIST'S RELATIONSHIP TO THE CHURCH – US:
Answer the following questions:

10. Eph.5:23 Christ is *HEAD OF THE CHURCH.*
     He is *SAVIOR OF THE BODY.*

11. Eph.5:25 Christ also *LOVED THE CHURCH*
     And He *GAVE HIMSELF FOR IT.*

12. Eph.5:26 to *SANCTIFY AND CLEANSE IT*
With the *WASHING OF WATER BY THE WORD.*

13. Eph.5:27 that He might present her to Himself a glorious *CHURCH* ... holy and without *BLEMISH.*

14. Eph.5:29 Christ *CHERISHETH AND NOURISHETH* the church. (ie, Us)

LESSON SIXTEEN
HOW TO KEEP YOUR SOUL ROOM OCCUPIED FOR LONGER PERIODS OF TIME

INTRODUCTION: Jesus said in Mt.5:48: "Be perfect as your Father in heaven is perfect." Jesus understands that we cannot live a life of perfection; but we can make it our goal to remain perfect for longer periods of time as we mature as Christians. Be wary of ever considering yourself perfect! This will immediately cause you to be guilty of the sin of pride.

Section One
THE FIRST STEP IN PERFECTION IS BEING BORN AGAIN:

1. John 17:23 Jesus spoke the following to His heavenly Father: I *IN THEM*, and Thou in Me; (why?) that they may be *MADE PERFECT* in one. ... (The Father and the Son can be in a person only when he has been born again.)

Section Two
ONLY CHRIST HIMSELF CAN BE PERFECT ON-GOING:

2. I John 1:8 If we say that we have no sin, we *DECEIVE* ourselves, and the *TRUTH* is not in us.

Section Three
HOW TO BECOME PERFECT FOR LONGER PERIODS:

3. Rom.12:2 Be not conformed to this *WORLD,* but be ye transformed by the renewing of your *MIND,* that ye may prove what is that good and acceptable and perfect *WILL OF GOD*. (ie, When your heart is being perfect, you will hear from the Father, do what He asks, and prove out His plan for the moment.)

4. Gal.3:3 Are you so foolish? Having begun in the Spirit, are you now being made perfect by the *FLESH*? (You cannot become perfect, even for a moment, by trying to do the do's and quit doing the don'ts. You become perfect only as you purge your heart/mind/soul by speaking words which cause the heart to be cleansed.)

5. 2 Tim.3:16-17 (Spend time in the Word because) all Scripture is given by *INSPIRATION* of God, and is profitable for doctrine, for *REPROOF*, for *CORRECTION*,   and for instruction in *RIGHTEOUSNESS.*

6. James 3:2 (Bridle your tongue to say only God-accepted things, for we all stumble in many things.) … If any man offend not in word, the same is a *PERFECT MAN*   and able to bridle the   *WHOLE BODY* (with God's help).

7. 2 Cor.7:1 (Let us learn God's promises and realize they can be ours and) let us cleanse ourselves from all filthiness of the *FLESH AND SPIRIT*, perfecting holiness in the *FEAR OF GOD*. (Again, this can be done only as you ask God's help in overcoming sin habits.)

8. 2 Cor.13:11 … Become complete by being of one *MIND* (with fellow-believers) and by (living) in *PEACE.* If you do these things, the God of love and *PEACE*   will be with you.

9. Heb.12:25, 28 See that ye   *NEGLECT*   not Him when He speakefh … . Let us have grace by whereby we may *SERVE GOD ACCEPTABLY*   with reverence and godly fear.

10. Heb.13:20-21 (May God) … make you   *PERFECT* in every good work to do (works spoken to you by the Father).

11. Col.3:14-15 Above all these things, put on *CHARITY*, which is the bond of perfectness, and let the peace of God   *RULE*   in your hearts, … and *BE YE   THANKFUL*.

12. James 1:4   Let *PATIENCE* have her perfect work, that ye may be

PERFECT AND ENTIRE, lacking nothing.

LESSON SEVENTEEN
GOD'S HIGHER PLAN REQUIRES FAITH - AND ACTING ON YOUR FAITH

INTRODUCTION: Paul tells us throughout His writings that faith is what pleases God – not works. James says that "faith without works is dead". So – to be a "Higher Plan" Christian, you must have faith and step out on your faith the instant He tells you to do so.

Section One
SCRIPTURE FROM PAUL AND JAMES:

1. Eph.2:8-9 (Paul wrote): By grace ye are saved through *FAITH* and that not of yourselves; it is the *GIFT* of God, not of *WORKS*, lest any man should boast.

2. James 2:19-20 (James wrote): Thou believest there is one God. Thou doest well. The devils *BELIEVE* and also tremble! But wilt thou know, … that faith without works is *DEAD?*

Section Two

3. Rom.10:9 If thou shalt *CONFESS* with thy mouth the Lord Jesus and shalt *BELIEVE* in thine heart that God hath *RAISED HIM* from the dead, thou shalt be saved. (ie, To believe is to have faith. To confess with your mouth is the necessary work.)

Section Three
JAMES OFFERS AN EXAMPLE OF FAITH WITH WORKS:

4. James 2:21-22 James wrote: Was not Abraham our father justified by *WORKS?* when he had offered Isaac his son upon the altar? Seest thou how *FAITH* wrought with his works, and by works, faith was made *PERFECT?*

5. James 2:26 James concludes: For as the body without the spirit is dead, so *FAITH WITHOUT WORKS* is dead also.

Section Four
A CLOSER LOOK AT JAMES' EXAMPLE:

<u>Abraham received His directions from God:</u>
6. Gen.22:1-2 And it came to pass after these things, that God (tested) Abraham and said unto him ... "Take now thy son, thine **ONLY SON**, Isaac, whom thou lovest, and get thee into the land of Moriah, and **OFFER HIM** there for a burnt offering. ... (ie, Abraham received his instructions from the mouth of God. We should do likewise.)

<u>Abraham obeyed exactly how, when, and where God directed:</u>
7. Gen.22:3(&4) And Abraham rose up early in the morning and saddled his (donkey), and took two of his young men with him, (as well as) Isaac his son. And he (split) the wood for the burnt offering, and rose up and **WENT UNTO THE PLACE** of which God had told him.

<u>Abraham spoke his faith before witnesses:</u>
8. Gen.22:5(&6) Abraham said unto his young men, "Abide ye here with the (donkey); I and the lad will go yonder and worship, and we shall **COME AGAIN** unto you."

<u>Abraham continued believing and speaking in faith:</u>
9. Gen.22:7-8 Isaac spake unto Abraham, his father, and he said, ... "Behold, the fire and the wood, but where is the **LAMB** for a burnt offering? And Abraham said, "My son, God will **PROVIDE** Himself a lamb for a burnt offering." So they went both of them together.

<u>Abraham believed God would raise Isaac from the dead if necessary:</u>
10. Gen.22:9(&10) They came to the place which **GOD HAD TOLD HIM OF**; *and* Abraham built an altar there and laid the wood in order; and bound Isaac his son and **LAID HIM ON THE ALTAR,** upon the wood.

<u>God will always come through when you obey Him:</u>
11. Gen.22:11-12 The Angel of the Lord called unto ... Abraham. ... and said, "Lay not thine hand upon the lad, neither do thou anything unto him; for now I know that thou **FEAREST GOD**, seeing thou hast not **WITHHELD** thy ... only son from Me.

12. Gen.22:13 Abraham ***LIFTED UP*** his eyes, and … behind him (was) a ram caught in a thicket... Abraham went and took the ram, and ***OFFERED HIM UP*** for a burnt offering (instead) of his son.

God will reward those who obey His voice:
13. Gen.22:18 (God said to Abraham): In thy seed all the nations of the earth (shall) ***BE BLESSED***, because thou hast obeyed My ***VOICE***. (We too are recipients of Abraham's blessings when we obey God's voice.)

Section Five
GOD PROVIDES HIS VOICE TODAY – AND MORE:

God provides His written Word to instruct us:
14. 2 Tim.3:16 All Scripture is given by ***INSPIRATION OF GOD***, and is profitable for ***DOCTRINE***, for reproof, for correction, for instruction in ***RIGHTEOUSNESS***.

God provides the five-fold ministry to teach us:
15. Eph.4:11 And (Jesus Himself) gave some (to be) apostles, and some prophets, and some evangelists, and some ***PASTORS AND TEACHERS***, for the perfecting of the saints, for the work of the ministry, for the edifying of the body of Christ. (us)

LESSON EIGHTEEN
GOD'S HIGHER PLAN REQUIRES THAT YOU KNOW THE PROMISES – AND REFUSE TO FEAR

INTRODUCTION: Fear is the opposite of faith. Fear is sin. What does the Bible tell us about fear?

Section One
YOU MUST NOT FEAR BECAUSE . . .

Fear is the opposite of love:
1. I John 4:18 There is no fear in ***LOVE,*** but perfect love ***CASTETH*** out fear; because fear hath torment. He that feareth is not made ***PERFECT*** in love.

2. I John 4:16 ... God is love, and he that dwelleth in love dwelleth in God, and **GOD IN HIM.** (The Spirit of Christ cannot remain in your soul room if love is not abiding there.)

Section Two
YOU MUST NOT FEAR BECAUSE . . .

Fear is disobedience to the Word:

3. Prov.3:25-26 (God's Word says): Be not **AFRAID** of sudden fear, neither of the desolation of the wicked when it cometh. For the Lord shall be thy **CONFIDENCE,** and He will keep thy foot from being taken.

4. Rom.8:15 Ye have not received the **SPIRIT OF BONDAGE** again to fear, but ye have received the Spirit of adoption whereby we cry, "Abba, Father."

5. Psa.91:5-6 Thou **SHALT NOT** be afraid for the terror by night, nor for the arrow that flieth by day, nor for the pestilence that walketh in darkness, nor for the destruction that wasteth at noonday.

Section Three
EXPECT TO BE FEARLESS IN EVERY SITUATION BECAUSE . . .

You have God's promises to stand on:

6. Psa.91:7 A thousand shall **FALL** at thy your side, and ten thousand at thy right hand; but it shall not come nigh thee.

7. Psa.91:10 There shall no evil befall thee, neither shall any **PLAGUE** come nigh thy dwelling.

8. Psa.91:4 (Expect God to) **COVER THEE** with His feathers, and under His wings shalt thou **TRUST;** His **SHIELD** shall be thy shield and buckler.

9. Isa.54:14 (Because) in **RIGHTEOUSNESS** shalt thou be **ESTABLISHED**; thou shalt be far from oppression, for thou shalt not fear. ...

10. Psa.91:9 Because thou hast made the Lord ... thy **HABITATION**.

Section Four
IN FACT – EXPECT TO BE HIGHLY COURAGEOUS BECAUSE . . .

God Himself is your protector:

11. Isa.43:2 When thou passest through the waters, (God) will be **WITH THEE**. And through the rivers, they shall not overflow thee. When thou walkest through the fire, thou shall not be **BURNED**, neither shall the flame kindle upon thee.

12. Isa.41:10 So…Fear thou not; for **FOR I AM WITH THEE;** Be not dismayed, for I am thy God. I will **STRENGTHEN** thee; Yea, I will help thee, I will **UPHOLD** thee with the right hand of My righteousness. (ie, Jesus Christ.)

13. Rom.8:38-39 For I am persuaded that neither death nor life, nor angels, nor principalities, nor powers, nor things present nor things to come, nor height nor depth, nor any other creature, shall be able to **SEPARATE US** from the love of God which is in Christ Jesus our Lord. (Principalities and powers are the demonic realm.)

LESSON NINETEEN
GOD'S HIGHER PLAN REQUIRES THAT YOU USE YOUR ARMOR

INTRODUCTION: Your enemy is looking for your weak point. He knows exactly what vulnerabilities you have, so do not give him an entry into your life. When the name of Jesus is spoken audibly, Satan knows he is a defeated foe.

Section One
SATAN IS YOUR ENEMY – MAN IS NOT!

1. Matt.5:44 Jesus said: Love your enemies, **BLESS** them that **CURSE** you, **DO GOOD** to them that **HATE YOU**, and **PRAY FOR** them which spitefully use you and **PERSECUTE YOU**.

2. Eph.6:12 Paul said: For we wrestle **NOT AGAINST** flesh and blood, but

against *PRINCIPALITIES,* against *POWERS,* against the rulers *OF THE DARKNESS* of this world, against hosts of *SPIRITUAL WICKEDNESS IN HIGH PLACES.*

3. Eph.6:17 So…take the *HELMET OF SALVATION* and the *SWORD OF THE SPIRIT* which is the Word of God. (ie, Keep your mind full of the Word and stayed on Jesus Christ. Then, when Satan either whispers his lies or attacks you, speak the Word and the name of Jesus. He will cower if you truly know the power in that name.)

<u>Section Two</u>
YOUR ENEMY IS SATAN WHO HAS MANY NAMES, INCLUDING THE FOLLOWING:

<u>Write the name(s) given to Satan in each verse:</u>

4. I Pet.5:8 *ADVERSARY; ROARING LION.*

5. Matt.12:24 *BEELZEBUB, PRINCE OF THE DEVILS.*

6. Isa.14:12 *LUCIFER, SON OF THE MORNING.*

7. Eph.2:2 *PRINCE OF THE POWER OF THE AIR, THE SPIRIT THAT NOW WORKETH IN THE CHILDREN OF DISOBEDIENCE.*

8. Rev.9:11 *ANGEL OF THE BOTTOMLESS PIT, ABADON, APOLLYON.*

9. Rev.12:9 *GREAT DRAGON, SERPENT, DEVIL, SATAN.*

10. Rev.20:2 *DRAGON, THAT OLD SERPENT, DEVIL, SATAN.*

11. John 8:44 *DEVIL.*

12. 2 Cor.4:4 *GOD OF THIS WORLD.*

13. Rev.12:10 *ACCUSER OF OUR BRETHREN.*

14. Ezek.28:14 ***THE ANOINTED CHERUB THAT COVERETH***. (This was his name before he was cast down.)

Section Three
WEAR YOUR DEFENSIVE ARMOR AROUND THE CLOCK:

Name the armor which covers each area listed below:

15. Eph..6:14   Around your waist (as your holster) you must wear what? ***TRUTH.*** ("Truth" is knowledge and wisdom coming straight from heaven. You can be most effective against Satan when you are following the Holy Spirit's leading.)

16. Eph.6:14b Over your chest area (as a breastplate) you must wear what? ***RIGHTEOUSNESS.*** (A proper breastplate will cover both your spirit and your soul. A person who has the Spirit of God in his born-again spirit and the Spirit of Christ flowing through his heart/mind/soul has on his breastplate of righteousness.)

17. Eph.6:15   What armor must you put on your feet? ***PREPARATION OF THE GOSPEL OF PEACE.*** (The gospel of Jesus Christ is a gospel of peace. Additionally, the Word teaches how to walk in peace every day. This, too, is the gospel of peace.)

18. Eph.6:17a What armor must you use to cover your head (ie, mind)? ***HELMET OF SALVATION.*** (Have your mind renewed daily by the Word. Be confident of your salvation and the faithfulness of God when you call on Him.)

19. Eph.6:16 Over your full suit of armor you must carry a shield which is called what? ***THE SHIELD OF FAITH.*** (When you have put on all the afore-stated, take up a strong shield off faith, trusting in the power and authority which is in the spoken name of Jesus.)

Section Four
CARRY YOUR OFFENSIVE WEAPON AROUND THE CLOCK:

20. Eph.6:17b What weapon must you use with great confidence? ***THE***

SWORD OF THE SPIRIT WHICH IS THE WORD OF GOD. (When Satan hovers, quote or paraphrase a verse from the Word of God and speak it with confidence, using the powerful name of Jesus.)

Section Five
SPEAKING THE NAME OF JESUS HAS GREAT POWER OVER SATAN BECAUSE….

21. Col.2:15   ….Jesus spent three days in Hades conquering Satan (when everyone thought He was lying dead in a tomb). While He was in Hades, He spoiled *PRINCIPALITIES* and *POWERS* (demons) and He made *A SHEW* of them openly, *TRIUMPHING OVER THEM* in it.

22. I John 3:8b Jesus came to earth in human form to destroy *THE WORKS OF THE DEVIL*.

Complete this sentence:
23. I John 4:4b When you use the name of Jesus, Satan has to flee, because *GREATER IS HE THAT IS IN YE THAN HE THAT IS IN THE WORLD.*

Section Six
SATAN RECEIVED HIS POWER BY DECEIVING EVE:

24. Gen.1:26 Satan wrested away the power which God had given Adam and Eve when He said: "Let us make man in Our image and let them have *DOMINION. …*

25. Gen.2:16-17 (God told His first couple): Of every tree of the garden thou mayest *FREELY EAT;* but of the tree of the *KNOWLEDGE* of good and evil thou shalt not eat, for in the day thou eatest thereof, thou shalt surely *DIE*.

26. Gen.3:6 (But after Satan came to Eve and enticed her), she took of the fruit thereof and did eat. She also gave it to her husband, and … he *DID EAT*. (At that moment, all of the dominion over the earth which God had given to Adam and Eve was given over to Satan's hand. He has had it ever since – except when we retake it using the name of Jesus.)

LESSON TWENTY
GOD'S HIGHER PLAN INVOLVES THREE STAGES OF SALVATION

INTRODUCTION: Christians speak of the new birth as "being saved" but that term is not entirely accurate. The new birth produces a new spirit in which the Spirit of God dwells. It requires only a moment to appropriate. You then have the remainder of your life on earth to accomplish the saving of the soul. A person can be confident of his eternal life once he has been born again, but additional great and glorious promises come with the life-long process of renewing the mind.

Section One

THE NEW BIRTH -- REGENERATION -- THE FIRST "SALVATION":

<u>Is a gift you receive when you believe and speak:</u>

1. Rom.10:9-10 If thou shalt **CONFESS** with thy mouth the Lord Jesus and shalt **BELIEVE** in thine heart that God hath **RAISED HIM** from the dead, thou shalt be saved. For with the heart man believeth unto **SALVATION** (of the soul), and with the mouth confession is made unto salvation. (The heart of a Christian is purged by the words of his mouth.)

<u>It is not a visible birth:</u>

2. John 3:3, 8 (Jesus said): ... Except a man be **BORN AGAIN**, he cannot see the kingdom of God. ... The wind bloweth where it listeth, and thou hearest the sound thereof, but canst not tell whence it cometh and whither it goeth; So is everyone that is **BORN OF THE SPIRIT.** (Just as the physical ear can hear the invisible wind, those around the new Christian will hear something new in him. He will speak differently as he tells of his new birth with joy

<u>It is eternal unless you renounce Him:</u>

3. John 3:18 He who believeth on (Jesus) is not **CONDEMNED**, but he that believeth not is condemned already because he has not believed in the name of the only begotten **SON OF GOD.**

4. John 3:16 For God so **LOVED** the world that He gave His only begotten Son, that whosoever believeth in **HIM** should not perish but have **EVERLASTING** life.

This first stage of salvation makes it possible (but not inevitable) to live an abundant, overcoming, and emotionally healthy life. It breaks the Father's heart that many Christians fail to move into the second stage of salvation – the renewing of the mind.

Section Two
RENEWING OF THE MIND – THE SECOND "SALVATION":

Call on the name of the Lord regularly throughout the day:

5. Psa.91:15-16 (God says through the words of David): He shall call upon Me, and I will ***ANSWER HIM***. I will be with him in trouble. I will ***DELIVER*** him and ***HONOR*** him. With long life will I satisfy him, and shew him My ***SALVATION*** (of the soul).

Ask for God's help in subduing old habits:

6. Rom.12:1 (As Paul said): I beseech you, … by the mercies of God, that ye ***PRESENT YOUR BODIES*** a living sacrifice, holy, acceptable unto God, which is your reasonable service.

7. Rom.6:19 … As ye have yielded your members servants to uncleanness, and to ***INIQUITY*** ... even so now yield your members servants to ***RIGHTEOUSNESS*** unto holiness.

Study the Word until you take on the attributes of Jesus Christ – The Word of God:

8. 2 Cor.3:18 We … beholding as in a glass the glory of the Lord, (through the Word) are (being) ***CHANGED*** into the same image from glory to glory, even as by the ***SPIRIT*** of the Lord.

9. Eph.4:21-23 If so be ye have ***HEARD*** Him (the Word and His voice) and have been taught by Him … (you will be putting)… off the old man … and you will be ***RENEWED*** in the spirit of your mind.

Expect life's circumstances to mold you into Christ's image – if you praise Him:

10. Rom.8:28-29 We know that ***ALL THINGS*** work together for good to them that love God, to them who are the called according to His purpose. For

whom He did foreknow, He also did predestinate to be *CONFORMED* to the image of His Son. … (God's plan paved the way for every believer to move to the higher level, but not all will. Will you?

Section Three
RECEIVING A GLORIFIED BODY – THE THIRD "SALVATION":
11. Phil.3:14 Paul said: I *PRESS* toward the mark for the prize of the *HIGH CALLING* of God in Christ Jesus. (ie, I press toward the higher level.)

12. Phil.3:20-21 For our conversation is (already) in *HEAVEN*, from whence also we look for the Savior, the Lord Jesus Christ, who shall change our vile *BODY* that it may be fashioned like unto His glorious body. (This is speaking of the glorified body which will be ours at the rapture and resurrection.)

Receiving a glorified body will complete our third stage of salvation. Praise God!

GOD HAS THREE IMMUTABLE REQUIREMENTS FOR ETERNAL LIFE

1. Jesus, the perfect Lamb, had to become a man and shed His sinless blood for your sins.
2. You must believe and confess that Jesus Christ is the Son of God, and that He rose from the dead.
3. You must continue to believe in Jesus and the sufficiency of His blood throughout your lifetime.

THEN, GOD HAS REQUIREMENTS FOR ADDITIONAL MAGNIFICENT REWARDS

4. As a Christian, you move into God's higher plan and become a recipient of His magnificent rewards – in this life and the next -- when you learn to practice the concepts in this workbook. BEGIN TODAY!

Other Bible study workbooks by Van and Barbara Ballew are:

Are You Equipped For the Work?
Believe To Receive! & Speak Or Leak!
Bible Study Made Fun!
God Looks On the Heart
Know the Fullness of "Christ"
Life Lessons From the Bible
Line Upon Line – Precept Upon Precept
Luke: The New Birth and Baby Christianity
The Rapture! Then What?
Understand the Bible Today
Whet Your Bible Appetite!
Teacher's Manual – Especially For Youth
Especially For Youth! (Books 1-4)

Made in United States
North Haven, CT
04 January 2024